'... words are simply inadequate to describe the horror, indescribable pain and continuing trauma of the community and survivors of Grenfell. But somehow in this searing and personal account from the moment the fire was raging, Alan Everett has managed to find the words and the wisdom to weave a profound story of suffering, community and the small beginnings of hope for something better. He uses his ministry and the scriptures ... to take us through anger, confrontation, community and sometimes irreconcilable differences in response to the black hell of the needless public incineration of so many people.'

Anna Ford, former newscaster and presenter

'... utterly faithful to the reality of what happened last summer, Alan Everett articulates the essential importance of the locally rooted faith and community institutions that emerged alongside an army of local volunteers to lead the relief effort in the total absence of any early official response ... Alan Everett's reflections on what it means to be parish priest, the richness of community relationships, the importance of solidarity in responding to trauma and beginning the process of healing contain lessons for all those engaged in local ministry, and demonstrate the unique ways in which a parish church can be equipped to do this.'

Lydia Rye, Senior Organizer, West London Citizens, Citizens UK

'*After the Fire* is a compelling, unsparing and scrupulous account of the Grenfell Tower disaster and its aftermath, informed by Alan Everett's commitment to the idea of the parish and the local. Essential reading for anyone concerned with the future of urban ministry.'

The Revd Donald Reeves MBE, Director of the Soul of Europe

D0234706

'Grenfell looms over our moral imagination as starkly as it does over the landscape of West London. Alan Everett was there, living and ministering in its shadow. In this short book, he walks us through the agony of the fire and its aftermath, and then explores what the fire shows us about faith, and what faith has to say about the fire. Moving, shocking, perceptive, honest: *After the Fire* is a beautiful reflection of a terrible moment in our common life.'

Nick Spencer, Research Director, Theos, the religion and society think tank

'Like the rest of the world I was both horrified by the Grenfell Tower tragedy and inspired by the gentle measures taken by the people of St Clement's on that horrible night. *After the Fire* is a sad but inspiring chronicle of the steadfast love of one small parish while all hell was breaking out around them. But it is also a powerful reflection on the role of the church in times of great calamity and a reminder to us of the mission of God's people everywhere.'

The Revd Dr Michael Frost, Vice Principal, Morling College, Sydney

'*After the Fire* is an important documentation of the tragic fire that engulfed the Grenfell Tower in the early hours of 14 June 2017. Alan Everett eloquently articulates the situation that changed the community in North Kensington. His book will remain an invaluable reference for researchers and for those interested in understanding the role of the community in responding to emergency situations.'

Abdurahman Sayed, Director of the Al-Manaar Muslim Cultural Heritage Centre

After the Fire

Finding words for Grenfell

Alan Everett

CANTERBURY
PRESS

Norwich

© Alan Everett 2018

First published in 2018 by the Canterbury Press Norwich
Editorial office
3rd Floor, Invicta House
108–114 Golden Lane
London EC1Y 0TG, UK
www.canterburypress.co.uk

Canterbury Press is an imprint of
Hymns Ancient & Modern Ltd (a registered charity)

Ancient
&Modern

Hymns Ancient & Modern® is a registered trademark of
Hymns Ancient & Modern Ltd
13A Hellesdon Park Road, Norwich,
Norfolk NR6 5DR, UK

978 1 78622 052 3

Typeset by Regent Typesetting
Printed and bound in Great Britain by
CPI Group (UK) Ltd, Croydon

For those who died
For those who are bereaved
For those who survived
For those who are haunted by memories

Contents

RESPONSE

Wednesday 14 June

The early hours

The sound of a helicopter overhead … Emergency vehicles on the street outside … Probably a police raid, I thought, before drifting back to sleep … Later … The helicopter still circling … Emergency vehicles still hurtling along the street … Vehicle after vehicle after vehicle … Why were there so many?

The doorbell rang. It was Sean Doherty, a priest who lives right by Grenfell Tower. He told me the tower was on fire. We set off, just before 3.00 am.

The walk up to Lancaster West Estate felt unreal. The street was deserted, eerily still. Then we saw the fire: raging, out of control. It leapt violently up the building, vividly illuminated against the night sky.

It was such terrible sight that I found myself struggling for a comparison, and rather pathetically came up with a film: *The Towering Inferno*. But this wasn't an act of the imagination. In that all-consuming fire beyond the police cordon, people were dying. It may not have seemed real, but it was.

I opened St Clement's church, turned on the lights, and lit candles on the altar, as a sign of God's presence and as an invitation to prayer. Then we went out to the police cordon, to find out how we could help. A few people were standing around in a state of shock. We asked some police officers where the evacuation centre was; one told us it was on Clarendon Road. Backtracking from the cordon, we reached Clarendon Road seven or eight minutes later. A small crowd was gathered under the street lights: sitting, standing, lying down. Most were silent; some were crying.

The scene was desultory and subdued. There were a few paramedics, and an ambulance, but this did not resemble a major evacuation centre. Where was everyone? *Or were these the only survivors?*

We met someone I knew, a tower resident. He had anticipated a disaster like this for years. The Grenfell Tower Action Group had repeatedly drawn attention to fire safety concerns, but it seemed no one had been listening. Wrapped in a blanket, he was calling on everyone around him to 'bear witness'.

Suddenly a group of kitted-up police officers appeared, marching along the road, down towards the tower. Someone called out, 'No, guys, don't! Take it easy, guys!' Then they were gone.

We decided to continue looking for other evacuation centres.

Heading back in the direction of the church, we popped into a community centre on Walmer Road: the Rugby Portobello Trust. A few people were carrying in supplies, but as nobody seemed to know what was going on, we returned to St Clement's.

Some people were already there. They had brought in water. We assembled tables, boiled as many kettles as we could find, got an urn working, put out tea bags, a jar of coffee, cups, sugar, spoons and found some milk.

Traumatized residents began to drift in. Some accepted a cup of tea. Most simply went and sat down. Volunteers arrived. A few were from the two parish congregations. One was from The ClementJames Centre, our sister organization – a charity serving the local area that originally emerged from a volunteer parish project. Others were from the wider community: I knew some, but not all. Everyone pitched in: pouring tea, offering biscuits, boiling more water, directing people to chairs and to the toilets. Firefighters came by.

A church member put a blanket on the floor, and set up a play area, using her own children's toys. A group of young Muslim men from East London brought blankets and clothing.

By 4.30 am, there were over 70 people sheltering in the church, and there must have been around 15 volunteers. Bread, biscuits and fruit were now piled up on the tables. Bottles of water kept on coming. We put out more tables.

As it was Ramadan and now daylight, many residents were fasting. They refused breakfast – even a cup of water – graciously, and without ostentation. I was concerned about their capacity to cope: how, in a state of shock, they would manage to get through the day ahead. We were only a week away from the longest day of the year. They would not break their fast until after 9.30 pm. As it happened, this was also the first of the most spiritually intense final ten days of Ramadan.

From 5.45 am, ClementJames Centre staff began to appear. Some carried supplies to firefighters and the police: out to the cordon and back, out and back, over and over again. Others started texting people they knew, to find out if they were safe.

At 7.15 am, feeling that I would be more useful if refreshed, I went home, for breakfast and a quick shower. It was strange walking out into the daylight, past the police cordon, and back along the busy street. People were moving urgently past me, towards the tower. Apart from a large number of stationary police cars, blocking the streets, there was virtually no traffic. The cordon had cut off commuter routes. We were in shut-down.

I ate breakfast watching the TV news. For over four hours I had been in practical coping mode, in the familiar territory of a small church. Now I saw the scale of the media interest. For the first time, I saw North Kensington through the eyes of the nation. Horrifying, hypnotic footage of the fire roaring up the tower constantly replayed, on a nightmarish loop.

The day unfolds

It was going to be a hot day. Outside, apart from the occasional sound of emergency vehicles, there was a strange quality of silence. People were hurrying towards the burning building, many of them carrying bottles of water.

A tall plume of smoke hung over the neighbourhood.

Back at church, the situation had dramatically escalated. There were many more helpers, and an increasing volume of donations: not only food and water, but also blankets and clothes. TV crews gathered outside, demanding interviews.

ClementJames Centre staff were controlling the church entrance on Treadgold Street, and the garden gates on Sirdar Road. It was hard, stressful work keeping the hungry media pack at bay, in an effort to protect desperate local people seeking shelter.

Members of the Kensington and Chelsea Tenant Management Organisation (TMO) arrived. The TMO was responsible for the management of the council estates. They sat by the main church door, taking down names. On several occasions, I was told to move out of the way.

In the melee, it was sometimes difficult to distinguish between evacuees, the bereaved, volunteers and journalists. The Centre offered the TMO laptops, so that data could be safely stored, but they preferred to use sheets of paper. In order to provide effective support on site, the Centre began to compile a spreadsheet – which the TMO then confiscated. They left in the evening, promising to return the next day. We never saw them again.

From mid-morning, it was almost impossible to do anything but react to the flow of people. Volunteers needed directing, the media was pressurizing us for interviews, and traumatized local people continued to seek support. The office phones were continually, relentlessly ringing. Most of the time, we were too busy to answer them.

The relief effort soon spread to the gardens and office spaces at the back of the church. Local restaurants and a coffee company brought in delicious, nourishing food. Enticing barbecue smells wafted across the garden. In the chaotic first phase of the relief effort, an estimated 2,000 meals were served – on both the church site, and down at the police cordon. Residents sat on garden benches for hours on end: dazed, numbed, shocked. The temperature soared and many sought shelter in the shade.

A volunteer medical station was set up in the church. In addition to conditions aggravated by the fire – such as asthma – prescriptions were urgently needed for evacuees from the estate who, in their rush to escape, had left behind their medical supplies.

Volunteers arrived in droves – including many from London churches – and donations rapidly accumulated. By the afternoon, the church turned into what one person described as 'the world's biggest jumble sale'; we were forced to put signs up around the church to say that we were no longer able to accept donations.

We only had space to store and distribute nappies, sanitary towels, toiletries and water. Other centres – such as Al Manaar Cultural Heritage Centre – were able to keep a greater range of items, which volunteers organized and passed on to those in need. By and large, however, local community organizations were overwhelmed by the goods they received.

It would have been a relatively straightforward task for the local council to identify warehousing, and to hire a fleet of transit vans to create much needed space by taking these donations away. The council did eventually help with their removal from our site, on the afternoon of Friday 16 June – very ably assisted by a diocesan contact. However, without private sector transportation and warehousing – arranged by the Centre – we would have been in desperate straits.

Over the first three days, we shipped out a vast quantity of unusable clothing – enough donations to fill three articulated lorries – mostly from St Clement's, but also from the other church in the parish, St James's. I will never forget the sight of dozens of heavy cardboard boxes being passed along a long line of helping hands into a lorry on Treadgold Street, cheered on by a crowd.

In the course of the day, some journalists tried sneaking into the church with donations, pretending to be volunteers. On one or two occasions, abusive members of the press had to be dealt with by the police. It is no wonder that for months afterwards many residents refused to be interviewed, believing that their trauma would only be exploited. As a result, others would step in and speak on their behalf.

We kept on expecting support and guidance from the council – perhaps someone with a walkie talkie, connected to a communication hub. But it never came.

Commercial organizations and many individuals offered accommodation. Entire hotels were available, but all these offers were rejected by the council, on the grounds of 'insurance' or 'health and safety'. Instead, traumatized evacuees would sleep that night on mats, on the floor of Westway Sports Centre. Even so, offers of accommodation circulated on site, and some were accepted by evacuees who preferred the comfort of a bed in a family home.

By late evening, a quality of calm – or was it exhaustion? – finally began to prevail. The last evacuees had left for the sports centre. A Ramadan 'break-fast' – an Iftar – was winding down in the garden, while in the church a group of volunteers was doggedly sorting through donations.

The church railings were covered with messages of solidarity, prayers and appeals for information about those missing. Flowers piled up on the pavement.

At midnight, I decided to close the church. No one needed a bed for the night. Our volunteers were worn out. But one resident thought we should remain open. She and her friends had just helped themselves to plates of hot food and were enjoying the community atmosphere. I knew I was going to have a problem when I heard her say, 'Man, I love this vibe.' It was frustrating finding myself in an argument with someone who seemed to think she was in the middle of an all-night party.

Closing-up took time, and it was nearly 1.00 am before I was able to lock the garden gates. Just as I was about to leave, a man pulled up in a van, coming forward with several bags. I explained that we were no longer receiving donations. Compared with some of the more aggressive donors we had encountered during the day, he was reasonable. He had come from outer London. His wife had sent him off at a very late hour to help, and would not be happy if he took back their offering. I was too tired to resist; his plastic bags joined a large pile in the garden.

Making my way home along the empty street, in the bleak and alienating artificial light, with the blackened and still smoking tower behind me, I passed photo after photo of those who were missing – pinned to trees or taped to railings and lamp posts.

It was like walking down a lost street with no future; a forgotten street in hell.

The burden of support

By 8.00 am the next day, many from The ClementJames Centre were already at work, along with **Into**University (IU) staff. The IU head office at St Clement's supports a network of centres throughout England. Unlike The ClementJames Centre, IU's focus is national rather than local. But you would not have known it. For weeks IU worked alongside Centre staff, putting in long hours, and dealing with very distraught residents. Both organizations suspended normal operations.

It was another blisteringly hot day. Two people were stationed with clipboards at both the garden gates and church door: controlling access, trying to protect vulnerable people from the press.

There were many other tasks: directing volunteers, working with those supplying meals, caring for the bereaved, attempting to liaise with other relief centres, disbursing money, coordinating a volunteer clergy rota for an impromptu Christian prayer room (alongside the Muslim prayer room), keeping the railings as tidy as possible, clearing away bags of rubbish outside the church and throughout the grounds, organizing useful supplies, staffing the reception area and, of course, trying to find a solution to the nightmarish problem of warehousing the donations that continued to pour into both churches. We identified something in the region of 18 task leaders that morning.

The Samaritans were an invaluable presence and support, staying on site for the next two weeks, and then returning whenever needed. From the very start, their contribution was outstanding.

As bad news filtered through, Centre staff found bereaved families quiet rooms in which to rest and mourn. My clergy colleague Mary Clarke remembers that Thursday as a day dominated by the sound of wailing.

The emotional burden of care was immense, for helpers from every organization. Over the summer, those in support roles were frequently traumatized themselves – either by what they saw on 14 June, or through the relentless pressure to respond to overwhelming distress.

On top of this, many staff members were themselves in mourning. Over 20 people known to those on our site had died – including children. Staff were forced to shuttle continually between practical problems and the needs of distraught residents, while all the time struggling with their own grief.

The last social media messages of some Grenfell Tower victims went out seconds before their death.

A national focus

In the first three days, there were a number of high-profile visits to the church. The most unobtrusive was the Archbishop of Canterbury: Justin Welby. He turned up unannounced to show his support. By contrast, the Leader of the Opposition and the Prime Minister arrived with a high level of security. Both visits meant we had to halt the relief effort.

The Prime Minister's visit posed a significant risk for the church and the Centre. We were a place of safety, a refuge, an oasis, but the feeling out on the streets was increasingly volatile; some described it as 'toxic'. Those guarding the entrance were battling not only with the press, but also with angry individuals: some trying to force us to accept donations we could not handle, others in a state of spiralling frustration. None of this was helped by the intense heat.

What impact would the Prime Minister's visit have on the calm and compassionate environment we worked so hard to create? The Conservative national government was inevitably identified by many in North Kensington with the Conservative council they felt had so badly failed them.

Mourning families were moved to concealed positions in the garden. We waited for a long time, with the media pressed up against the railings. The Prime Minister's route in through the back door of the church was seen by some as a covert action, but it would have been far too dangerous for her to have used the front entrance.

Theresa May's time at St Clement's turned out to be a useful listening exercise, but it was cut short by turmoil out on the street. She left quickly through a hostile crowd. Some shouted, 'Murderer!' and tried to attack her.

We ran the serious risk that this meeting would create a rumour that we were colluding with distrusted authority figures. The merest hint that we were working against the interests of local people would have been devastating. We had to retain the trust of the community. More than that, we had to deepen that trust: to work with the angry and grieving.

The Prime Minister's visit highlighted a tension between the national and local church. The national church had a mediating role, while at St Clement's we had a pastoral and representative role. The furious crowd could easily have turned on us. As far as I know, only one person appeared on television to criticize the decision to allow the Prime Minister on to the premises, but he may have been speaking for others.

This issue was very much on my mind as a hastily formed group of residents, volunteers and staff was driven over to Downing Street on Saturday 17 June, to continue the conversation. One member of the group did not want to go through the front door. She was not sure she had a mandate to represent her community. I chose to accompany her through the back entrance – partly as an act of pastoral support, and partly because I wanted to protect the unobtrusive ministry of the parish.

The meeting lasted an hour and a half – much longer than we had expected. Residents were able to describe their experiences, and to voice their concerns. The failures of the council, the chronic inefficiency of the TMO, and decades-long underfunding of social housing were all put on the table. This useful meeting contributed to the Prime Minister's decision later that day to send in a Task Force, to take control of the disaster response.

Residents subsequently issued a press statement. Those most directly affected by the fire spoke with their own voice. After an initial facilitating role – the meeting was chaired by the Bishop of Kensington – the Church of England stepped aside.

In the fast-moving first few days, routes for dialogue were quickly formed. Back channels were set up between key local representatives and the newly appointed government Task Force, and the highest levels of government.

St Clement's became a useful environment for meetings and conversations. The Centre's media blackout enabled vitally important mediation work to develop, away from cameras and the glare of publicity. By contrast with later public meetings, these private, small-scale encounters were focused and constructive. From the earliest days, trusting, supportive relationships were formed between Centre staff and survivors, other residents, and the bereaved. These relationships would continue to deepen, enabling traumatized people to speak to those in positions of power.

Groups that met on the site would decide how and when they wanted assistance. Attendance at closed meetings would be by invitation only. If someone had a bright idea, an offer of help, or a request for an interview, the Centre would pass on the message, but that would be all.

The Centre works directly with over 2,600 people each year. But from now on, there would also be a large number of people urgently seeking Grenfell-related support. The commitment of the staff was extraordinary, and the quality of their response outstanding.

Meanwhile, back in the church gardens

While the meeting at Downing Street was taking place, the Centre was running another event, in the church garden. This was the weekend of the Great Get Together: gatherings inspired by the memory of MP Jo Cox, on the first anniversary of her murder. The Centre went ahead with its plans for a picnic, with a focus on children's activities. In a similar fashion, the parish stuck to its planned events: a bowling trip for young people the following Saturday, and a week after that the summer fete.

Former Centre staff, friends and volunteers turned up to help, along with those who had been working flat out for the gruelling past three days. There was an awkward moment before the event began, when some confrontational people appeared at the garden gate, but it was soon dealt with.

The Get Together was profoundly restorative. Children – and adults – were given a chance to forget the horrors they had seen. While their faces were being painted, they were able to discuss the 'big fire', freely admitting it had been 'scary'. The art therapy sessions offered that afternoon would soon become a vitally important outreach initiative across the area, enabling children to access their feelings before they became too deeply internalized. It would be difficult to overestimate the contribution made by the 'watchful waiting' of art therapists.

Activities included mask-making, table-tennis, and an opportunity to learn how to play the steel pan. However, a project to record what people valued about their community – planned before the fire – had a sombre new resonance; many found it too difficult to participate.

Around 100 people attended the event, including regular Centre clients, those who had sought refuge at St Clement's, and those passing on the street. Free pizzas were provided by a national chain. For three hours, out in the sunshine, in a lovely, restful garden, residents had a moment of relief from the trauma they had experienced.

Sunday Mass

By the weekend, there was an attempt by community organizations to 'normalize'. Of course, the very idea was delusional. It was far too early for 'business as usual'; and anyway the community would never be 'normal' again.

Even so, we fought to regain a vestige of control. For me, this was nowhere more necessary than at the first Sunday service after the fire: at the 11.30 am Parish Mass. With some significant further assistance from the private sector, on Friday afternoon the council finally contributed to the removal of boxes piled high in both churches. Members of the two congregations then set about preparing for Sunday worship. However, they could do little more than throw sheets over the five second-hand fridges that had somehow been left behind. Those fridges were of no use whatsoever to survivors living in temporary accommodation, and as a gesture of support they were massively inappropriate, given it was thought that a fridge had started the fire.

On Saturday evening, I had a call from the diocesan press office to say that the Mayor of London wanted to join us at St Clement's, but his team had concerns about his safety. This was largely because of the angry reception the Prime Minister had received outside the church the previous day, although he too had been heckled on an earlier visit to the area. I assured the press office that the Mayor – Sadiq Khan – would be warmly welcomed. We did not receive the final confirmation that he was coming until Sunday morning. I found out on my return from a 7.00 am live interview on the BBC *Sunday* programme.

There was never any doubt about the type of welcome the Mayor would receive. The congregation loved having him with us. His attendance, together with his wife, was a profound and sensitive act of solidarity. He spent a considerable amount of time after the service listening to people, including many who had lost close friends in the fire. He knew victims by name. And there was a lighter side to the occasion. Dozens of young people had their photos taken alongside him. Their beaming faces told us just how much they looked up to him. He was a role model. A Londoner, a Muslim, of Asian background, he represented the city they knew, someone they could admire and possibly emulate. His presence with us brightened their day, providing a brief moment of forgetting.

Before the service, there were only one or two photographers outside the church. By the end, they were there in force. Speaking to them as he left, the Mayor promised that he would be 'a fighter' for the residents.

The Mass itself was intensely moving. Approximately 150 people were packed into the small church. The atmosphere was subdued, attentive. From the moment we stood for the opening hymn and prayers, there was a palpable sense of unity. The sermon, preached by Robert Thompson, part-time priest in the parish and a Labour councillor in Dalgarno Ward, spoke of an inherent brutality in our social system, with its disregard for the poor, and quoted Pope Francis:

> The Gospel tells us constantly to risk a face-to-face encounter with others, with their physical presence which challenges us, with their pain and their pleas, with their joy which infects us in our close and continuous interaction. True faith in the incarnate Son of God is inseparable from self-giving, from membership in the community, from service, from reconciliation with others.
> (*Evangelii Gaudium* 88)

The sermon may have provoked strong feelings among some members of the congregation, but whatever anger they felt, it was contained. There was then an emotional transition. We stood for two minutes' silent prayer. Immediately afterwards, virtually everyone came forward to light a candle in sand trays positioned around the church. There was a deep sense of release as, for some, this was the first time they were able to weep. The mutual support in those few minutes was transformative.

The structure of the liturgy enabled us to feel that the chaos of the situation – the turmoil of our feelings, the overwhelming sense of grief and loss – was in some small way being expressed in a safe place before God.

Towards the end of the service, the Bishop of Kensington – the Rt Revd Graham Tomlin – paid tribute to the faithful service and witness of the parish community, over very many years. Bishop Graham had been a tireless presence in our midst for the past few days – and would continue to provide energetic support in the coming months.

As soon as the Mayor left, I checked my phone. There was a message from the Chair of the St James's Garden Committee, to say that the drains at our other church – St James's – had exploded. I rushed down to find him in overalls and wellington boots, attempting to mop up the overflow. A smell of sewage pervaded the gardens, where another Great Get Together picnic was about to take place. He promised to arrange for emergency assistance.

I popped round to the event's organizer. While we were talking, I realized to my acute embarrassment that my black clerical shirt had an elaborate tie-dye effect, caused by salt stains from dried perspiration.

She sent me home with a bottle of wine.

A failure of communication and support

During the week beginning 19 June, relief centres found ways to work together. And yet there was still no real public information system – and never would be. In time, a daily news sheet would appear, but its impact was limited. Why weren't large digital public information boards immediately stationed around Notting Dale? Why wasn't Text Local used?

There were no information sharing protocols in place, and this made it difficult for centres to provide coordinated care for survivors and the bereaved. It would be many days before ID numbers were issued. Police liaison officers were appointed but, again, communication was poor. Everyone understood that in most cases it was too early to say who had died, but relatives were not even told whether or not the missing were in hospital. That information was readily available. Instead, families were left in a distressing state of uncertainty.

Banks either refused outright to release significant sums of money to community centres, or did not have enough cash at local branches – even though organizations such as The ClementJames Centre and Rugby Portobello Trust had received large charitable grants, to enable survivors to meet their basic material needs.

Banks should now review how they respond to emergencies. In times of crisis, they are not simply commercial organizations, but part of a public relief effort.

Widening circles

As we entered the second week, support services became increasingly focused and streamlined. The official death toll was rising, and people were beginning to lose hope that their relatives were just 'missing'. Places of worship and community centres were essential places of refuge.

There was a new tenderness in the air; friendships were intensified. This quality of gentleness was apparent in the contribution by a man called Richard. He travelled each day to be with us, from some distance away. At first, no one quite knew why he was cutting up empty plastic water bottles. Then we saw that he was making improvised containers, for the flowers out on the street. He attached the containers to the church railings, to create a beautiful display. As flowers continued to arrive on site, he made new containers and kept them all watered. He did this for several weeks, preserving flowers that otherwise would have died in the baking heat.

We also felt a strong sense of togetherness at church. The congregation at St Clement's is local: most live on the surrounding estates. Families had been evacuated;

some – especially those with children – had decided they were never going to return. Recurring sounds and images afflicted a large number of residents. As we gathered on Sunday mornings, a quality of shared fragility was all too apparent. No one was surprised by sudden emotional reactions.

In the course of those first few weeks, we received a number of visitors at the Sunday Eucharist. Some popped in, after spending time reading the tributes and the appeals for those missing on the railings outside the church. Others made a special journey to be with us.

Led by Andrew Willson, the church began to offer a vigil every Monday evening, and this continued until December. People came to light candles, to experience a few moments of peace and quiet, in an intimate and prayerful space.

However, communication with the outside world was problematic. Local faith leaders were concerned that if they did not speak to the media, other unrepresentative and self-appointed figures would take their place. In the autumn, the parish's renewed engagement with the press created an issue for The ClementJames Centre, as it had committed itself to a media blackout. Not everyone understood that the church and the Centre were different organizations, with different roles and responsibilities within the community.

Even so, talking to the media – in time – seemed the right thing to do. Faith leaders were in a position to act as advocates. Public sympathy for residents fluctuated over the first six months. Some felt that the survivors were being given too much, and that there was an over-emphasis on the fire, as opposed to other major incidents, such as the terror attack at the Manchester Arena in May 2017, when 22 people were killed, and over 500 injured. Others exaggerated the extent of outside political inter-ference, which had the effect of minimizing the depth of feeling in North Kensington.

Faith leaders were able to speak about the suffering they encountered, to help create a bridge between those most affected and those further away, to bear witness to what the community had experienced, and underline the wider implications of the disaster. For example, at the invitation of Prince Harry, Abdurahman Sayed, the CEO of Al-Manaar Cultural Heritage Centre, delivered BBC Radio 4's Thought for the Day on 27 December. This was one of many occasions when local faith leaders tried to deepen understanding, and to promote a culture of sympathy and respect. The impact of these interventions may have been minor, but we felt that any attempt to keep the issue alive was important.

However, the media often wanted a simple summary of what 'the community' was feeling. This raised the thorny issue of representation. We had to be careful to ensure that we spoke only about what we knew. Journalists would sometimes want to be put in touch with survivors from the tower. But in the early days the majority were far too traumatized to deal with the press. On the whole, survivors did not come forward until four or five months after the fire, by which time many others had spoken on their behalf.

There was no single 'community' of North Kensington: no one voice, no one perspective, but a multiplicity of voices: often very angry. This anger became increasingly apparent in public meetings held throughout July and August.

Intended as opportunities for the sharing of information with residents, those chairing the meetings struggled to keep control. The first meeting was held at Al-Manaar, the second at St Clement's. As the YouTube heading of a recording rightly observes, it ended in chaos. Thereafter, the heavy burden of public meetings was mostly shouldered by the Notting Hill Methodist Church, and it subsequently became the venue for the highly fractious Grenfell Recovery Scrutiny Committee meetings. The church had a clear view of Grenfell Tower, and was a natural gathering point. The minister, Mike Long, soon developed a significant community role.

On a rising tide of feeling, questions at those summer meetings were thrown at the police and other statutory authorities. Each answer provoked a flurry of further questions, often at the same time. Those present wanted to know how many had died, when the final figure would be released, how many people had been in the building, why the investigation was taking so long, why it was proceeding as it was, how many had been brought in by the police for questioning, why no one had been charged with murder, when evacuees would be rehoused. They raised concerns about money, about the quality of key-worker support for survivors, about air quality and many other matters.

The inadequacy of building regulations, the process leading to the choice of flammable cladding, the council's attitude towards the estates, government social housing policy and a host of other issues were repeatedly raised, in these meetings and elsewhere.

However, within three months of the fire, some wealthier residents of the borough began to say that a 'them and us' attitude had emerged, with no apparent recognition that thousands of residents had been traumatized: both survivors from the tower and others.

We need to remind ourselves what we are talking about here. We are talking about those who stumbled over bodies as they struggled through heavy smoke in a state of terror down the single staircase, those who barely survived, those forced to watch the fire on the night, those who lost relatives and friends, those who exhausted themselves frantically searching for missing relatives, those who endured weeks of not knowing what had happened to the missing, those who heard people screaming, those who received graphic and harrowing final social media messages, children who discovered empty places in their school classrooms, those whose balconies were covered in the debris that rained down from the tower, those whose doors were broken down, those who returned to neighbouring flats to find that there was no gas, those who would never be able to return to their flats, those who were evacuated to hotel rooms with distraught children, those many hundreds who were unable to sleep, who relived the event over and over and over again.

The first-hand trauma was extensive, and there was also the second-hand trauma experienced by those trying to help them, for whom the experience of listening and trying to provide some kind of support was exhausting.

The list of things to be angry about was extensive: the provision of only a single staircase in the tower, the absence of a fire escape, cheap cladding that went up in flames as if petrol had been thrown on it, inadequate building regulations, no sprinkler system, no safe spaces within the building, the poor quality of care by the TMO, fuelling speculation that the council had a hidden agenda of wanting the estates to fall into such a state of disrepair that they would have to be 'regenerated' (to include private housing), the initial advice from the fire service on the night of the fire to 'stay put', and an inadequate access area for fire emergency vehicles, further hampered by the illegal parking of cars. And this list was by no means complete.

Anger can be a challenging emotion, and some of those lamenting the emerging 'them and us' attitude may have been feeling defensive. Many residents on the estates also found the anger difficult. At the furious public meeting at St Clement's church, a number of distraught local people left, unable to cope with the level of verbal violence.

The disaster attracted people from outside the area, some of whom addressed the meetings, their contributions adding to the distress of residents. Demonstrations at the Town Hall, with a strong presence of political activists, raised the emotional temperature even higher.

Yet some wealthier residents in Notting Hill or Chelsea were startled to see the people of North Kensington in a state of emotional turmoil, speaking about their marginalization. In one sense, this was only to be expected; many from the 'south' rarely went 'north'.

By contrast, residents in the south of our parish – around St James's Gardens – were both appalled and sympathetic. Their response to the disaster was in some cases very generous. They were bewildered that a council that had seemed to be doing its job well had responded so poorly in the terrible first few days. Some would have housed survivors, if the council had seen fit to accept their offers.

As the vicar, I became a messenger, conveying news of the relief effort to those who wanted to help. At a couple of public events, I was asked to step to the front and speak. I was applauded – not for any eloquence on my part, but simply because people wanted to show support.

The Holland Park environment in the south of the parish was itself useful. Our summer fete in St James's Gardens – thankfully, no longer smelling of sewage – was a wonderful, happy distraction, just over two weeks after the fire. Working with the PTA of our church school, the fete gave a welcome reprieve to a fantastically diverse gathering of over 500 people, many of whom were still in a state of shock. The Garden Committee later opened the gardens to survivors, for private gatherings.

The complaint about a 'them and us' attitude was made by people who felt less personally connected. But this was not the only self-centred response to the catastrophe. Far worse, as far as residents were concerned, was the 'grief tourism' that began on a large scale from the very first day. Some visitors were respectful, others less so, taking 'selfies' in front of the tower.

A busy summer

In the days and weeks following the fire, we witnessed an ever increasing number of people wanting to get involved: sharing their opinions, offering help. North Kensington was awash with activists, lawyers, counsellors, journalists and other commentators. There was an outburst of creative activity: music, visual arts, film, poetry.

Community centres reached out to one another. The different faith groups began to talk and share, and gathered for a series of interfaith acts of remembrance over the summer. Doors of communication opened, although there was often too much information to absorb: about the latest developments, the latest initiatives. Suddenly everyone was attending meetings, but it was hard to know how well the survivors and other residents were being supported.

Underlying all these divergent responses was an impression of acute anxiety. The pandemonium of the first few weeks may have subsided, but on a daily basis community centres were still being faced with a long list of urgent and unpredictable problems. Everyone felt as though they were 'stumbling through the dark' or 'making it up as we went along'.

Offers of help kept flooding in. All these had to be assessed; many were unsuitable, or too early in the grieving process. What did people really need, and how should limited resources best be directed? The consequences of appointing the wrong partners would be devastating: badly damaged people would be hurt even further by inappropriate or incompetent support, and yet proper provision had to be made, under significant pressure.

Some community activists were hardly sleeping. WhatsApp messages would be sent in the early hours of the morning. Residents were confused about what services were on offer. Even those only slightly away from the disaster sometimes felt it would be wrong to ask for help, in case it displaced those in 'greater need'.

Throughout the summer, The ClementJames Centre focused on trips and events, offered well-being clinics and NHS drop-in support, as a prelude to the more in-depth counselling that would become available from late August onwards. A parish pilgrimage to Salisbury also provided a welcome moment of respite.

The hot summer gave some people the space they needed, and in early August there was a significant multi-faith vigil at the base of the tower. Representatives from a wide range of faiths affirmed their solidarity with all those who were suffering, and pledged their commitment to uphold the community. Messages from survivors and the bereaved were carried into the tower. The event was respectful, dignified and moving.

A strange combination of disorientation and volatility prevailed until the Notting Hill Carnival, in the last weekend of August. There had been some concern about the carnival. With feelings running high, there was a real possibility it might become a focus for unrest. Some wanted the carnival to be stopped, as a sign of respect for those who had died, and their families. In the event, an element of respect was incorporated, in an act of remembrance at the beginning of the first day, and through an appeal for quieter behaviour on the section of the route closest to the tower. With exceptional weather, improved administration and a very strong police presence – all were in body armour – the carnival ran fairly smoothly.

The trauma deepens

The changing season, and the beginning of a new school year, helped to create a sense that things were 'moving on'. For those with children, there was a new sense of purpose. However, this was only on the surface; for many, September was the point when the reality of the situation really began to sink in. The adrenalin that had powered them on through the summer finally ran out. They were overtired, and felt frustrated and impotent. Some were signed off work.

Schools – an important source of support for young people – had to resume as normal, in the full knowledge that many in their community had died, or were in mourning. Kensington Aldridge Academy, at the foot of the tower, had relocated to a temporary site by Wormwood Scrubs, close to Burlington Danes Academy. It was not at all clear when it would be able to return, as the school had been overwhelmed by debris from the fire.

Trauma counselling can only begin to be effective from roughly two months after an event; late August and early September represented a transition away from psychological first aid. The need was there, it was widespread and emerging with force, but it would be quite some time before most found the right kind of support. Meanwhile, people were experiencing mood swings, sleeplessness, and a crushing sense of powerlessness. A mood of resignation masked many problems.

The underlying causes for the anger expressed at the summer public meetings had yet to be addressed. Most evacuees were in hotel rooms, and only a small proportion of residents were accessing counselling services. There continued to be mixed reports about the effectiveness of the survivors' key workers. Many flats in the walkways below the tower were still without gas. (A situation that lasted for months.) That part of the estate resembled a ghost town.

Living with a daily view of the blackened tower was very difficult – especially for those who saw it each morning as they opened their curtains, or raised their kitchen blinds. Many people kept them closed. Parents began taking their children to school by a different route, in an attempt to avoid it.

The tower could not be covered. As it was being viewed as a crime scene, changes to the atmosphere had to be avoided. However, this meant that on windy days, material continued to fall on neighbouring flats. One resident told me that months later she found blue paper on her balcony; on closer inspection, this turned out to be wallpaper.

The 'recovery process' was painstakingly slow. There was widespread anger at the absence of arrests. The lack of clear information about how many had died was distressing. The final death toll of 71 only appeared in mid-November. A further survivor, Maria Del Pilar Burton (Pily), died in hospital on 29 January 2018; I officiated at her funeral.

As autumn wore on, the sense of communal togetherness began to dissipate. Residents in different blocks received different treatment – in relation to housing and money – and not all these distinctions seemed fair and just. Some were apparently coping better than others. Some had resolved their practical problems, while others had not. These variations sometimes led to resentment; and when neighbours fell out, they had nowhere else to go. They kept on bumping into one another.

Residents associations were attempting to function in a situation that showed no sign of improving, and they had no effective means of engaging with the council. There appeared to be no strategic plan.

And so throughout October and November, despite the wonderful work that so many were doing, anger that previously had been directed at the council began to surface between neighbours. There seemed to be no end to the pain. Everyone was locked into a situation that they could never have envisaged, and which few outside the area appeared to understand.

By the end of the year, a large number of evacuees were still in hotel rooms, or in temporary accommodation, and there was no timetable for taking down the tower. Some survivors had been arguing that it should remain standing until guarantees had been obtained from the council and government about how the land on which it stood would be used. Others felt it should stay in place as an indictment of incompetence and neglect. However, the daily psychological damage it was inflicting on residents was unacceptable.

The provisional findings of the Inquiry into the causes of the fire would not be released for many months – and in addition to this, many were frustrated that local people were not going to be given an advisory role. Problems remained with counselling referrals; and NHS projections suggested that too few people were coming forward for help.

Despite every effort to address the needs of local people, despite heartening stories of good neighbourliness and mutual support, despite the courage and resilience of so many, and significant acts of solidarity, such as the St Paul's Cathedral Grenfell Tower Memorial Service on the six-month anniversary of the fire, the community was paralysed.

With so much uncertainty, and in a state of such deep helplessness, it was hard to be optimistic about the New Year.

Yet for many, 2018 couldn't come fast enough.

REFLECTION

Faith in community

In the summer of 2017, it became apparent that places of worship potentially have a significant role in a crisis – providing they have made a strong commitment to neighbourhoods, to the small scale, to life below the radar.

If so, their value consists principally of three things: first, their readiness to respond, as an integral part of the community; second, their ability to elicit trust through a recognized history of engagement; and third, their capacity to become places of sanctuary and refuge.

Again and again, the media returned to the story of how faith groups stepped up to meet the challenges of the Grenfell disaster, working alongside other community organizations.

Their story captured the public imagination, but we now need to take a step back for reflection, in order to establish some underlying principles for this type of ministry.

Partners in community

When I opened up St Clement's church in the early hours of 14 June, and turned on the lights, it felt as if my working life as a priest had found its most coherent expression. I still find myself wondering why.

One explanation relates to symbolism. An open door is a potent symbol of welcome, of hospitality. We generally expect churches to be inviting places of community and worship. Sermons focus on the need for hospitality and inclusivity. We try to ensure that a visitor's first experience of a church is a positive one. Healthy churches usually work hard to ensure that everyone feels able to participate. All these tasks involve a commitment to keeping 'doors open'.

While the 'open door' is a routine feature of parish ministry, it has a biblical resonance. Jesus described himself as 'the door', and urged people to 'knock, and the door will be opened for you'. A closed door is so antithetical to our understanding of our mission and ministry that it almost seems to be anti-Christian. And yet, as we saw in the weeks after the Grenfell fire, a closed door is sometimes essential: giving people privacy and sanctuary when frightened, distressed, or need to discuss sensitive issues. In general, however, the open door expresses a core value.

Light is an even more dominant image in Christian narrative. We say that Jesus is the Light of the World. Candles in church remind us of this, but they also have a looser significance.

Around the world, the act of lighting candles at vigils has become a common way of expressing grief, prayer and hope. It is a natural and easily accessible symbolic gesture, regardless of faith. Perhaps its power has something to do with the early days of our species, when fire brought people together, giving them comfort, warmth and protection from the surrounding darkness. Children – and some adults – are often afraid of the dark, needing the reassuring presence of a night-light.

The turning on of lights in the darkness is a highly visible gesture of availability. It says, 'We're here to help.' The light blazes forth, and those in need know where to go. Conversely, lighthouses warn ships of imminent danger. Lights show us the way. But in this context, on this particular night, there was more.

St Clement's is a small church, tucked away from the main roads through North Kensington, nestled among large estates of social housing. It is one of the relatively few architecturally significant buildings in Notting Dale.

Many people know of Notting Hill and its carnival. But the 'Dale' – just down from the 'Hill' – is another matter. The boundaries of Notting Dale are not all that clear, and the term is oddly pastoral. But the Dale is where St Clement's church can be found – with some difficulty – and where for decades congregations have attempted to live out their Christian faith, and to serve the wider community.

One hundred and fifty years ago, Notting Dale was an area of terrible poverty, even by Victorian standards. St Clement's church was built by the Revd Arthur Dalgarno Robinson: a mission church in the best sense of the word, serving both the material and spiritual needs of the inhabitants. His name was eventually given to a council ward a little further to the north, in an area of still significant deprivation.

The social gospel this initiative embodied continued in various forms into the twentieth century, and was given fresh impetus in the late 1970s and 1980s. In 1992, a community development project was founded as a separate charity from the church, which later became known as The ClementJames Centre. The Centre is a secular organization, but the partnership between the church and the Centre has always been strong.

From 2002, The ClementJames Centre developed highly successful programmes for improving the opportunities of young people and adults. In 2007, this led to a sister charity (**Into**University), which expanded the young people's programme beyond North Kensington. In the meantime, The ClementJames Centre has greatly extended its own range of services for adults as well as children – building on its early achievements to become a highly respected and successful local charity. The achievements and growth of the national charity **Into**University have been equally impressive.

Consequently, when I opened the church that Wednesday, I wasn't beckoning people into a building that was in any way disconnected from the community, or into the building of an isolationist sect, or into a building where the problems of poverty and social exclusion had been spiritualized. Quite the reverse. I was inviting them into a building with a tradition of service that stretched back 150 years.

At 3.00 am, I hadn't yet grasped what it would mean to be at the centre of a mass disaster. I was struggling to make sense of what I was seeing. My reactions were confused. I knew the church was needed, and that I had to do what I could to ensure it responded in the best possible way. But the burden was not entirely mine. At that moment, I felt as if I was in the presence of all those who had worked and worshipped in the church before me.

Many volunteers arrived at St Clement's in the devastating first three days. The parish office received hundreds of letters, often with cheques or cash enclosed. I was deeply moved – and encouraged – by their messages of goodwill. I felt as if I were being supported in a real, practical way by prayer offered from around the world.

Those writing to us frequently said that their offering was 'small', but hoped it would be 'of some use'. Their emails and letters gave a different picture of the church from one that sometimes circulates: of an inward-looking club, doomed to extinction by its lack of relevance. If a desire to help others is so deeply felt, the church will surely survive and continue to make a meaningful contribution, whatever the future may bring.

However, the narrative initially told within the wider church was not always completely accurate. It spoke of 'the church' rallying round, or of 'local churches' opening their doors. While both these statements were true, they did not represent the whole truth. The name of the Anglican parish church – St Clement's – was in some instances barely spoken. This may have been because in the immediate aftermath of the fire there was an urgent need to affirm the wide-ranging nature of the response. But whatever the reason, it took a while for St Clement's and other front-line places of worship to be named, along with community centres and schools. The real story was only gradually 'fleshed out'. Even so, some contributions have yet to be recognized – and perhaps never will be: either because the media inevitably has to simplify, or because some people work more effectively from places of obscurity.

All photos by Matthew Barrett

Pages

1   The deluge of donations, piled high inside and outside the church.

2&3 The Sunday Eucharist after the fire.

4   Floral tributes, 'missing' notices, prayers and mementos.

Partnerships were crucial; and this was underlined in The ClementJames Centre's Winter Newsletter, issued in mid-December:

The ClementJames Centre has resumed its day-to-day operations whilst still providing support to the constant stream of survivors and directly affected residents. This includes emotional and wellbeing support, assistance liaising with the council and other relevant services, assistance with grant applications, as well as trips, events and activities for affected families.

To ensure we provide the best support possible, we have been working in close partnership with a range of specialist organisations, including mental health and trauma charities Place2Be, Child Bereavement UK and Winston's Wish, who have been offering informal counselling to children, young people and parents at our centre. For many weeks the NHS also offered drop-in sessions at ClementJames for local residents to discuss their physical and emotional health needs. Since the beginning of the new academic year, Latimer Community Art Therapy have been running art therapy alongside our Academic Support sessions.

Throughout October, ClementJames staff were processing survivors' applications for financial support from Family Action. Most recently, we have been processing ticket applications for the Grenfell Memorial Service at St Paul's Cathedral, and are planning a trip to Winter Wonderland for 150 directly affected residents. Overall, ClementJames has supported over 200 affected households to date.

We continue to work closely with survivors group Grenfell United and have been hosting community lunches for them in partnership with local business Cru Kafe. Local residents are invited to join us to watch a live screening of the St Paul's Memorial Service in St Clement's church on 14th December at 11am.

This report gives us a glimpse of the networks that sprang up. But community centres had to make careful judgements about potential partners. They had to learn quickly about trauma, and as each mass disaster is unique there were no 'off the shelf' models to work from.

The defining characteristic of the Grenfell Tower fire was that it was not inflicted by a terrorist group, but from within a system of local governance, and that it occurred in a disadvantaged area with high density housing. The context was complex, and the pastoral needs were diverse and widespread. Many of those who needed help already had significant problems. Speakers at the summer public meetings often demonstrated a deep sense of disempowerment, and a complete loss of trust.

The pressure to create a responsive environment of care was intense and unrelenting, and continued for months. Normal activities were displaced, and only began to be resumed in September.

Church and Centre

St Clement's church has been open for public worship for 150 years, offering sacraments and pastoral rites, and a range of support programmes. No doubt it was a source of comfort for many during the two World Wars. It has often been used as a space for public meetings, and is available for community use today. It is a place of quietness and healing, and offers a sense of continuity; all the more necessary in a large, impersonal city such as London.

Over the years, community centres, places of worship and other local organizations have proliferated in North Kensington. In the aftermath of the disaster, they made complementary contributions to the recovery effort, and began to work more closely together.

At their best, partnerships have a mutually reinforcing character. We had already noticed this in the relationship between the church and The ClementJames Centre. A survey of local attitudes undertaken a short while before the fire reached what might have seemed to be a counter-intuitive conclusion: that trust in the Centre's wide-ranging and ambitious community work had been deepened by its association with the church.

We might have expected a different conclusion: that the church connection would raise concerns about motive. We might have expected the survey to show that the Centre needed to distance itself from the church, in order to be clear that it had no hidden agenda, no desire to proselytise.

What the survey actually revealed was that the church connection works to the Centre's advantage. Many local people have great affection for St Clement's. For generations, the church has been present at key moments in their lives: at marriages, baptisms and funerals. These rites often involved an extended family network. As in other parishes, this cumulative pastoral reach has been unseen and can all too easily be underestimated. At the same time, many in the neighbourhood have attended the church school – from grandparents down to small children. Quite a number have fond memories of their time as altar servers.

In return, the church benefits from its association with the Centre. Families from a very wide range of backgrounds feel completely at home on the site, largely because of the immensely valuable work the Centre has been doing for the past 15 years.

A virtuous circle of trust has taken both organizations deep into the community. As a result, in the aftermath of the fire people of all faiths, and none, not only sought help, but also worked alongside us as volunteers – including those from the Muslim community, which suffered such grievous losses.

Meanwhile, St Clement and St James Church of England Primary School has for decades made its own vitally important contribution, nurturing local children in a distinctively Christian but inclusive environment.

Like other organizations, the church is part of an extensive network, which extends ever outward. The sum of the whole is far greater than its individual parts. One term for this mysterious accumulation is 'incarnational ministry'.

System breakdown

In the aftermath of the Grenfell fire, like many others, I found myself struggling to regain a sense of control; the council's lack of readiness for the emergency plunged us all into chaos. If a disaster plan had been written, there was no impression that it had ever been rehearsed. St Clement's became a relief centre by default – simply because we were near the tower and had opened our doors. The council seemed to have no idea what to do with us, and at one point even tried to close us down – at 7.00 pm on 14 June, when many people were still on site, and looking forward to an evening meal, or the Ramadan Iftar ('break-fast'). I had to go around issuing a counter-notice, emphasizing that people were welcome to stay for as long as they wanted.

The church is a significant public building, and the Centre is a major focus for community work, but we had never been involved in emergency planning. The situation would only gradually begin to acquire any semblance of order from the Saturday onwards, when the Prime Minister sent in a government Task Force, after condemning the council's response. For three critical days, the distress of the bereaved, survivors, and other residents was immeasurably deepened.

In the wake of this systemic collapse, I found myself struggling to clarify the role of the church. I felt the need to tell its history and explain why it was able to respond as it did. To this end, I wrote an article for *The Church Times*, which went online on Monday 26 June.

This might seem quixotic: surely I had better things to do with my time? Perhaps, but along with many others I found that an already acute sense of helplessness was aggravated by well-meaning but sometimes misdirected attempts to help, or worse, to tell our story for us.

Over the following weeks and months, I began to reflect on some core assumptions and beliefs. Why was the parish system important? Was it merely a means by which the church could organize mission and ministry, or was something more involved? Was it increasingly out of date, or did it have something important to tell us about the nature of God?

Having worked for a large part of my adult life as a parish priest, I have a huge investment in parish ministry. Like many others of my generation, I have been saddened by its apparently irreversible decline. Before the Grenfell fire, I assumed that I would see out my last few years before retirement, trying to be as effective as possible, while feeling that the church into which I had been ordained – in 1985 – had changed so much that I was a bit like an old dog that probably couldn't be taught too many new tricks.

The fire forced me to take a closer look at what I had been doing throughout my working life, beginning with a concept that emerged with its foundational significance intact: the incarnation of Christ.

The incarnation

For Christians, the incarnation is an empowering sign of God's identification with humanity. It is at the heart of all our caring, our outreach, and in the partnerships we form with others – not least in parish ministry.

The image of God as a vulnerable baby, in a displaced family, acquires a new meaning when we think of those who fled terrified from the burning building. The story of that small child, so much in need of love and protection, stands as a sign of judgement against the abuse and neglect of all vulnerable children of God. The nativity, with its imagery of a family exposed to the elements, seeking shelter, underlines a basic human fragility, shockingly exposed in the presence of death.

The Grenfell catastrophe helps us grasp the human cost behind every two-minute news clip: a cost that if anything escalates after the media interest has moved on. It suggests that a revolution in thinking would be required for us to take suffering seriously. Were this to happen, we would become a society with fundamentally different values, and a radically transformed sense of purpose.

The majestic prologue to John's Gospel (John 1.1–14), heard to such dramatic effect each Christmas, palpably evokes the enduring and sustaining presence of God. The darkness of the world is real, and acknowledged, but even so, 'The light shines in the darkness, and the darkness did not overcome it.' The Gospel writer speaks with the authority of a personal encounter: 'And the Word became flesh and lived among us, and we have seen his glory, the glory as of a father's only son, full of grace and truth.' When we hear these words, we search in our minds for those occasions when we too have seen the glory of God.

The parish system at its best is an active expression of this incarnational principle: of God's identification with us, as a light in the darkness. God's presence in the Middle East 2,000 years ago guarantees God's presence every-where for everyone. It is as if the past continually and indiscriminately seeps into the present. In the aftermath of the Grenfell fire, the outworking of the incarnation was a matter of supreme importance, and at the heart of everything we did.

Many years ago, when visiting Nazareth, I went for a walk in the surrounding countryside. It was deeply re-assuring to think that I may have been walking in Jesus' own footsteps. I felt as if I were absorbing through the shared earth something of his hidden, private life as a child and young adult. The experience made him seem at once a historical person and a universal, contemporary figure: as if he were walking beside me.

Of course, on a rational level, the idea was a fantasy: the actual soil would have been different. But for me, the land was infused with a vivid, encouraging presence.

A well-known poem by William Blake captures this sense of connection, and relates it to social transformation:

> And did those feet in ancient time
> Walk upon England's mountains green?
> And was the holy Lamb of God
> On England's pleasant pastures seen?
>
> And did the Countenance Divine
> Shine forth upon our clouded hills?
> And was Jerusalem builded here
> Among these dark Satanic mills?
>
> Bring me my bow of burning gold;
> Bring me my arrows of desire;
> Bring me my spear – O clouds, unfold!
> Bring me my chariot of fire!
>
> I will not cease from mental fight,
> Nor shall my sword sleep in my hand,
> 'Till we have built Jerusalem,
> In England's green and pleasant land.
> (William Blake, Preface to *Milton*, 1804–8)

Blake begins by offering two images of presence: first, of God walking in paradise (Genesis 3.8), applied here to

England's 'mountains green' – and second, of 'the holy Lamb of God', in England's 'pleasant pastures'. These two images, with their pastoral overtones, are so appealing that we are almost led to believe that God may indeed have once walked about in England. But then doubts appear: 'And did the Countenance Divine' really shine upon our 'clouded hills', and was 'Jerusalem builded here / Among these dark Satanic mills?'

Following on from this menacing image of exploitation, Blake fervently declares his intention to use all the powers at his disposal to build the heavenly city in England's 'green and pleasant land'. He demands a 'bow of burning gold', 'arrows of desire'; and he calls down a chariot of fire such as the one featured in Elijah's ascent into heaven (2 Kings 1.12).

The fourth stanza is an impassioned statement of dedication to imaginative activism – to unceasing 'mental fight' – and this activism is partly driven by the very real possibility raised in the first stanza: that God may once have been seen in England. The Garden of Eden, the incarnation and a vision of a new social order cohere, as the poet commits himself to work towards the new Jerusalem of Revelation 21.1–3.

The darkness of contemporary England is so oppressively evoked that it almost negates the hopeful possibilities of the first stanza. Yet they linger, and so there is a powerful, enabling ambiguity at the heart of this great poem.

As a hymn, these words are powerful not only because of Hubert Parry's stirring music, but also because we too find ourselves moving between a lament at the assault of destructive forces in our society, and a desire to effect positive change, convinced that this change is possible, in part because God may already be in our midst.

As few of us have Blake's capacity to see the world as both profoundly lost and innately transformable, we tend to lapse into banal narratives about whether the place where we live is 'safe', or 'nice', or 'friendly'. The cosmic process of reconstruction to which Blake commits himself seems a world away from the concerns that normally shape our thinking about local issues: such as our job, our family life and relationships, the property market, the condition of housing estates, levels of crime or the quality of schools and hospitals.

But we do sometimes find ourselves thinking two things at once in relation to the incarnation. On the one hand, we inhabit a faith tradition that places great importance on the idea that 'those feet once walked here' – and if not directly here, somewhere else on earth, and somewhere we may conceivably visit ourselves. But on the other hand, we often subscribe uncritically to the assumption that our society is fundamentally secular. Yet many people not only paid tribute to the faith community's response to the Grenfell disaster, but also turned up to help. They immediately recognized that we had a significant contribution to make.

Seen in this light, our anxiety that in some way 'God has left this place' may well be something of an overreaction. Census statistics about the decline of church affiliation and attendance are obviously very worrying. However, we must be wary of overgeneralizing. Churches in poor urban areas such as Notting Dale sometimes saw the decline much earlier. Speaking in 2017 to a priest of the parish from the 1950s, it seemed that our levels of Sunday attendance were surprisingly similar.

But the more general point is that when we reflect on the incarnation we are brought to the paradox so powerfully expressed in Blake's poem. It seems almost impossible for us to believe that Christ lives here among us. The incarnation was an event that happened over 2,000 years ago, and so much of our society is heading in such a different direction that it seems pointless looking for signs of it today. Yet, belief in the incarnation sustains us, and as we 'incarnate' this belief in the way we live, it acquires demonstrable significance.

It is sometimes said that the theology of Anglicanism can be found in its worship; that on the whole Anglicans do not go in for systematic theology, but for faith as it is lived and practised. It could equally well be said that the theology of Anglicanism – at least in the Church of England – can be found in its parish system, with its implicit commitment to binding together the wider community.

The Trinity in every parish

The virtues of tolerance, inclusivity, service, outreach to those in need, of seeking God in the beauty of worship, in music, in the arts – all these and more are understated theological values, telling us something about what many believe to be the nature of God. This view of God, so characteristic of liberal Anglicanism, is at its best profoundly Trinitarian: speaking of God as creator, God living among us, God guiding us forward.

A fundamental insight arising from any doctrine of creation is that each neighbourhood – area, parish – is a gift from God. This gift includes previous generations of Christian witness and service, and inevitably at least one church building, but the gift is greater than this. It includes every aspect of local life, which on arrival we seek to understand, in all its idiosyncrasies, with all its strengths and weaknesses, all its achievements and challenges.

The claim that each parish is a divine gift may seem far-fetched, but it follows on naturally from the assertion that we are made in the image of God. This image is waiting to be unveiled, in numerous contexts, within every community. It may be deeply hidden or it may lie just beneath the surface, but it is there. There is no place that is Godless. When we arrive in a new place, we find that God is there before us; it is God's place before it is ours. Recognizing that we are being entrusted with a gift in creation – whether in parish ministry or elsewhere – is the first step in any act of Christian service, witness, ministry or mission.

Second, Christ is among us, having in some way renewed and restored the image of God. According to Matthew 25.31–46, he is encountered in those most in need: the hungry, the thirsty, the stranger, the naked, the homeless, the sick and the prisoner. Christ is also to be found in baptism and the Eucharist, as well as in the other sacraments of the church. We hear his words in Gospel readings, and he is communicated to us through sermons. In the Eucharist we take his very being into ourselves.

Third, the Holy Spirit offers us reassurance and comfort, while helping us to break free from the prisons in which we find ourselves: of narrowness, prejudice, judgementalism and rigidity. The Holy Spirit gives us the energy to change, the courage to reach out to others, and the wisdom to discern the right way forward.

This, at least, is the theory, but the problem is never in the theory, but in the practice. In run-down urban contexts, a parish may at times feel more like a gift from a malevolent enemy than God. It may feel more like a site of chaos than order. It is never easy seeing Christ in the angry and disappointed person on the doorstep who doesn't want yet another bloody cup of tea and a cheese sandwich, but cash. And church councils struggling with decaying buildings and intractable financial problems may be forgiven for wondering from time to time whether the Holy Spirit has decided to leave them for a more fruitful mission field.

At times, parish ministry feels like a tremendous privilege; at other times, an impossible challenge. But it is precisely because the uncertainties and frustrations are so real that Christ's incarnation matters: as both a reassurance and an inspiration. In the aftermath of the Grenfell fire, this sign of God's commitment to us was even more necessary and sustaining.

In one sense, the incarnation reveals what was already the case: that God loves and cares for us. But it was – and is – more than that. It is a covenant, a binding agreement. We are helped towards a better understanding of what this might mean by analogy. Every child is loved by God, but in baptism a commitment is made on both sides. We meet Christ in many ways, but we encounter him profoundly in the Eucharist.

In the incarnation a new sign of presence was given, enabling us to see the world around us in a different light, and drawing us towards the imaginative transformation of which William Blake spoke: to play our part in building 'Jerusalem', wherever we may be.

Yet the incarnation is not only something external to us, as a sign or an agreement, but an actual and specific act of union. Paul's description of sexual union as the creation of 'one flesh' (1 Corinthians 6.16) takes us a step further towards understanding the baffling mystery of the incarnation; and this type of language is validated elsewhere, when Paul uses marriage (including its consummation) as a metaphor for the union between Christ and the church (Ephesians 5.22–32).

Christ's death on the cross is sometimes described as a 'bridge' from fallen humanity to God. But this diminishes the significance of the incarnation, and turns his birth, maturation, and ministry of teaching and healing into little more than a prelude to the real drama of salvation.

A more holistic view of Christ's life is that the 'bridge' moment occurs at the incarnation, when Christ becomes 'one' with us. This 'oneness' is deepened in his torture and death, when he absorbs a terrifying level of violence, and experiences despair. In his resurrection and ascension, he then 'takes us up' into God.

The Christian creeds assert that Christ's birth, death, resurrection and ascension were a 'once and for all' historical event. At the same time, the circular movement of descent and ascent, in which we are taken up, is re-enacted today – to a great extent, through the sacraments of the church.

The incarnation and the sacraments are part of a continuum, in which the physical world is part of a sacred network: apparent in water, oil, light, the sign of the cross and human touch. However, an even more intimate quality of bodily connection is experienced in the Eucharist: when Christ comes to us in bread and wine.

A sense of place

The incarnation is both our context and mandate for building networks and working alongside others. It reinforces our understanding of each place as part of an inherently sacred created order, and as a site of potential transformation.

In view of this, a neighbourhood may be many things, but it is never going to be a blank sheet. The construction of the 'new Jerusalem' will inevitably be with local materials. Or to put it another way, the image of God in creation will not be imported, but revealed.

It is easy for a newcomer to a neighbourhood to underestimate the bonds that already exist: to overlook the small ways in which they create a sense of community, however tenuous. In poor urban settings the very fragility of these bonds underlines their significance. To minister sensitively in this context we need to be humble and careful.

Before arriving at the parish of St Clement and St James in 2010, I worked in Hackney, in East London. During my 17 years there as vicar, that part of Hackney became progressively more gentrified. However, in many respects the parish remained the same: the majority of residents still lived on council estates. But they were invisible to some newcomers.

In contexts like these, parish churches provide a valuable opportunity for enabling people to meet one another: to reveal the real nature of the place, to humanize the environment and to promote social cohesion.

Everywhere in apparently rootless urban contexts, there are invisible people: people who have been there all the time, but have been discounted. They are often poor or socially excluded in other ways: perhaps because of age, disability, faith, ethnicity, sexuality, gender or mental health issues. However, the pressure on resources, and the struggle to keep 'the show on the road', can mean that unassuming and under-confident vulnerable people are overlooked.

Jesus seems to have responded to those in need without an ulterior motive. The many stories of healing in the Gospels tell of Jesus' naturally responsive compassion. Modelling ourselves on Jesus, we are called to make practical and compassionate care an end in itself, while rejoicing in any spiritual benefits that may unexpectedly result. A key sign of the priorities of any congregation is its attitude to the rites of baptism, marriage and funerals. How seriously are they taken, and how much is expected in return? How inclusive is our pastoral ministry?

It is easy when arriving in a new neighbourhood to over-look the potential for community-making from within. When I first moved to my current parish, I found it frag-mented. In my previous parish, I was constantly meeting people I knew. Here, I hardly saw the same people from one day to the next. Or so I thought.

Seven years on, I can see how wrong I was. Even so, it took me quite a while to develop relationships, even from my socially privileged position as a vicar. But the parish church system, embedded in the community, offers one means of enabling those street-level acts of recognition and engagement to take place. They are all too easily undervalued. It is astonishing how much our sense of place changes when we find ourselves greeting someone in the street, or when we see others doing so. Such acts of recognition are disproportionately powerful signs of a relational potential within an otherwise anonymous context.

When I think of North Kensington, I think of a place where the web of friendship is spread as thinly as in any other city environment, but even so this sense of con-nectedness is very important. Centres of worship and local community organizations have helped to sustain it for decades, working unobtrusively against loneliness and isolation.

Pubs used to be extremely significant. With their closure, a community focus has largely been lost. To a small ex-tent, local shops have helped fill the gap. For a pensioner who lives alone, the simple act of popping into a shop to buy a pint of milk may provide an opportunity to make contact – especially if she is recognized. Leisure centres are potentially an even greater source of support, enabling people not only to keep fit, but also to make friends. The new leisure centre just below Grenfell Tower has been a support and a blessing for many in the neighbourhood.

In the days and weeks following the fire, we faced the prospect of compound trauma. Not everyone who was traumatized was lonely, vulnerable and poor, but many were. And so places of worship needed to be accessible to everyone. They needed to be recognized places of safety and nurture and to offer pastoral care without an ensuing sense of obligation. Those who turned up for help needed to find themselves in the presence of others like themselves, to whom they could easily relate. In times of crisis, places of worship – and community centres – are ideally both *in* and *of* the areas they serve.

The idea of itinerant ministry, so important in the earliest years of the church, must be balanced by a fully developed concept of rooted ministry. After only a very brief period of coexistence with their fellow Jews, the first Christians were ejected from synagogues, and their connection with Jerusalem was broken. The Gentile world became their primary mission field. We have a radically different context, in which the church has been present and active for centuries. We should acknowledge that reality, and continue to work up from existing foundations.

Who is my neighbour?

There is no doubt that a long history of ordinary, life-sustaining bonds helped to carry the community through the terrible aftermath of the Grenfell Tower fire. Jesus' answer to the question, 'Who is my neighbour?' never seemed more pertinent.

Today, those preaching about the parable of the Good Samaritan (Luke 10.25–37) have to underline the hostility that in Jesus' time existed between the Jews and Samaritans. Jesus' shaming of Jewish religious leaders who fail to help a badly wounded traveller would have been pointed enough without the figure of the Samaritan, a despised outsider. Offering a Samaritan as a model of good neighbourliness would have chastened and perhaps also angered the lawyer who questioned him.

Nothing like this level of antipathy existed in North Kensington between different groups, religious or otherwise, but while there was goodwill, relationships were largely undeveloped. Most organizations worked more or less independently from one another. In the aftermath of the Grenfell fire, new and vital partnerships emerged.

The parable of the Good Samaritan was told in a sectarian context very unlike North Kensington. Even so, it is a sharp reminder of the necessity of learning from the contribution of others to the common good, especially those with whom we do not think we have a natural connection.

It is possible to envisage an alternative version of this story, in which a number of travellers are violently assaulted, and the Samaritan and the Jewish leaders come together to help them. In this new narrative, a shared act of assistance brings the helpers closer to one another.

This was our experience in the aftermath of the Grenfell disaster.

The question, 'Who is my neighbour?' – and Jesus' answer – relates directly to the incarnation. God thinks communally, crossing the divisions we create. My neighbour is not only the person I seek to help, but also the person who works alongside me – who is both my neighbour, and my partner in service.

However, it required a careful process of discernment to identify suitable partners – especially when considering offers from outside the area. Relationships had to be developed, with both commitment and insight. As in every neighbourhood, this remains an ongoing task.

Solidarity in suffering

The incarnation is rooted in the idea that human life is sacred, not only because God is our creator, but also because Christ was born and lived among us. The gift of the Holy Spirit at Pentecost may be taken as a further sign of God's commitment to our flourishing, as we seek to move forward in mission and witness. But our definition of 'mission' can easily become too narrow, isolating conversion from well-being. Service and prophetic witness provide a scripturally rooted corrective, in which the call to justice, care for the poor and faith are intertwined.

When we think about Christ's provocative ministry, it seems almost inevitable that he would be put to death. He spoke truth to power with such authority – by word and symbolic action – that his opponents were bound to respond ruthlessly. He courageously bore witness to his teaching about the nature of God as compassionate, freely accessible, eternally reaching out to heal and liberate us, all the way to an agonizing execution.

The nature of his death has pastoral as well as prophetic implications. The cross signals God's solidarity with us in suffering. Like many others, whenever I take the sacrament of Holy Communion to people at home, I set out a small statue of the crucified Christ. This visual sign reminds us that Christ is present whenever we feel at our weakest. The cross invites our gaze, asking us to come to God in our vulnerability and helplessness.

Good Friday worship connects our experience of suffering with Christ's self-sacrifice; the resurrection hope of Easter springs from a terrible abyss. Whereas much of our time is spent in an emotional and spiritual middle zone, the transformative power of Holy Week and Easter depends on a stark contrast between darkness and light. Few of us would want to pay the mental health toll that would be exacted by continually shuttling between despair and exhilaration. In any case, it would impede us in the business of daily organized living. But we do need the emotional and spiritual stretching that Holy Week and Easter provide.

A few years ago, during a visit to the Taizé community, I was struck by its version of 'the veneration of the Cross'. Each Friday and Saturday, the community re-enacts Good Friday and Easter. Saturday evening is very beautiful: hundreds sit together in the large church, holding candles and singing. But the Good Friday liturgy is truly extraordinary. At the end of evening prayer, when the Brothers leave, the large free-standing Taizé cross is placed on the floor. The worshippers – mainly young – then shuffle forward on their knees.

Those at the front of the queue gather round, and place their heads on the icon. It is a comforting, trusting group activity, expressing something of the call to bring our burdens to Christ, who will give us rest. There is no hurry to move on. On my visit, the first group stayed in position for several minutes, while hundreds patiently waited and chanted.

Those in line were doing something outlawed at the Reformation: moving on their knees towards the cross. Significantly, this modern version of the banned medieval custom of 'creeping to the cross' was not introduced by the Brothers, but spontaneously by young people themselves. They instinctively found the appropriate way to pray to the crucified Christ.

My trip to Taizé coincided with a large number of Lutheran visitors, from Scandinavia and Germany. Some waited on their knees for well over an hour to take up their position. This Good Friday style ritual has a sustaining and deepening power that reaches across denominations. The universal appeal of Taizé is evident from testimonies by young people on the Taizé website. The experience of staying at the community can be profoundly restorative, not least because it introduces silence into lives driven by social media.

Contemplating the cross while music is being played or sung can be a powerful experience. However, we usually view the cross in quietness. The cross creates a space where we can place our needs, our anxieties and our grief. It has the capacity to open up a deep, hidden place within us, a place that in the usual course of events we may find difficult to access. Entering into this hidden, sometimes dark space is potentially therapeutic, providing we can be certain that we are being safely held.

It has often been noted that the cross only became a widespread Christian symbol after Constantine abolished crucifixion in the fourth century. Jesus' followers would have been traumatized by Christ's unexpected and gruelling death, and persecution and martyrdom was a recurring experience for the first Christians living under the Roman Empire.

Grenfell Tower has shown us how disturbing a site of violent death can be. In the aftermath of the disaster, the blackened hulk felt unreal. We could hardly believe that we were looking at a place where so many perished, in agony and terror. For residents, the tower was a daily act of visual abuse, taking them back to the night of the fire. Even those travelling through the area were shocked. The tower reeked of violence. Some felt it had a menacing presence, as if it were alive.

The tower has helped us to understand how distressing the sight of a cross would once have been – evoking brutality and oppression – before it eventually became an enabling symbol of God's sacrificial love in Christ.

In order to exercise its healing power, the cross must not act corrosively on our imagination. While speaking of a particular event in a specific time and place, it must also be capable of absorbing what we bring to it. Yet for some, the crucifixion can all too easily reawaken memories of trauma, or even worse, appear to sanction it. At a subliminal level, the cross may be received as a message about the inevitability of victimhood. The cross has the capacity to induce fear at the prospect of random, denigrating acts of brutality – either as a punishment for sin, or as a test of faith.

Self-sacrifice is still widely regarded as a heroic act of virtue. The respect shown over and over again in North Kensington towards firefighters makes this abundantly clear. Although the term 'martyr' has become linked to terrorism, the idea that people might bear witness to God or a higher value in their death still has consider-able appeal, as we see in services of remembrance, not least for those who have died in war; and their death can lead to change. For example, the memory of those lost in Grenfell Tower will continue to be a potent call to action on social equality.

However, the language of sacrifice that permeates both the Old and New Testaments has a different resonance for many of us today, for whom the shedding of blood is no longer seen as a necessary transaction. Even so, Christ's sacrifice was real. He accepted a terrifying and painful death in order to challenge the abuse of power, including the abuse of religious power. His death laid the foundations for a radically different view of social and political hierarchy, and we are still on a journey to bringing that vision – a vision of the kingdom of God – to fruition.

Christ's self-emptying

Employing the words of an early Christian hymn, Paul speaks of Christ 'emptying' himself to become human:

> Let each of you look not to your own interests, but to
>   the interests of others.
> Let the same mind be in you that was in Christ Jesus,
> who, though he was in the form of God,
>   did not regard equality with God
>   as something to be exploited,
> but emptied himself,
>   taking the form of a slave,
>   being born in human likeness.
> And being found in human form,
>   he humbled himself
>   and became obedient to the point of death –
>   even death on a cross.
> (Letter of Paul to the Philippians 2.4–8)

Christ's self-emptying – his 'kenosis' – in order to become a 'slave', involves the surrender of his divine attributes. He would not have been fully human if he had retained the omnipotence or omniscience that are essential features of God. But it could be said that there are two further aspects to his kenosis.

The appalling anticipation of our own death is something we continually have to manage: in effect, to repress. But as we grow older, or as we encounter terminal illness, this act of repression requires considerable psychological energy. It might be said that we only begin to acquire wisdom when we stop struggling against the knowledge of our mortality, and try to live with it, however imperfectly. Those who have come to accept the fleeting nature of existence have a perspective from which we can all learn.

Like us, Christ must have experienced stress, frustration, exhaustion, confusion, a debilitating sense of incompleteness, and the fear of pain and death – both in the Garden of Gethsemane and at other points in his life. Had he not, he would not have been fully human. But this is not to say that he lived in sin, and we should not view those times when we experience these things as signs of our unworthiness, or our sinfulness. They are simply indications of our need for God's grace.

Christ subjected himself to all this as an act of identification with us, and then accepted its intensification in his passion and death, leading to his agonized, despairing cry from the cross: 'My God, my God, why have you forsaken me?' (Mark 15.34; Matthew 27.46; cf. Psalm 22.1). Whereas Christ willingly embraced emptiness, in order to be one with us, the challenge for us is not to embrace emptiness as something *foreign* to our nature, but to acknowledge it as *intrinsic* to our nature. Only when we have done this, can we begin to function as self-aware human beings who recognize that we are loved by God as we are, in our incompleteness and anguish, and not as we would wish to be.

The embrace of the incarnation was seen by early Christian teachers as a way of taking us into God's own nature. In the words of Athanasius: 'For He was made human that we might be made God' (Section 54, *On the Incarnation*). Some Eastern Orthodox theologians contrast the 'exchange' of divinization, of 'theosis', with the 'transaction' at the heart of the Western church's theories of the atonement.

Christ's passion and death have an essential part to play in this exchange. To conceive of a God who overpowers all opposition would encourage us to value aggression, dominance and unreflecting action. In the vulnerable figure of Christ, who absorbs the evil inflicted on him, we are given another set of values, and a different type of language. For the first Christians, this signalled an end to the need for temple sacrifice: one aspect of atonement theory we can unreservedly endorse today.

Jesus accepts the apparent collapse of everything he has worked for. He does not resist those who arrest him. He submits to interrogation, torture and a painful, humiliating death. He becomes a weak, reviled object. He experiences psychic disintegration. And so we are invited to think differently about failure. The exchange of emptiness for fullness, of humanity for divinity is not a simple, rational choice of the obviously more beneficial option, but a difficult decision, which requires us to discover within ourselves a capacity to trust in God despite the odds, perhaps even despite the evidence we see before us.

Very few of us manage to do this with any consistency. Our journey to God is slow and halting. We experience the process of 'divinization' most intimately in the Eucharist, when we receive the body and blood of Christ. The connection established at this point is real, but at the same time it is a token of a future union we can only glimpse.

In trying to accept that we are fundamentally and continually in need of God's grace, we start to notice the temptation to take short cuts. We are encouraged to become more humble, more compassionate towards ourselves, and more realistic about our limitations. We become more open to partnership with others: more able to see them as fellow travellers.

In order to work with God towards the immensely ambitious project of universal divinization, we need to see ourselves in history. Even the Incarnate Christ could not anticipate the outcome of his self-emptying. He depended – and still depends – on others to carry his mission forward. In the same way, we each make our contribution, only to be succeeded by those who follow us. The salvation of the world does not depend on us, and we cannot anticipate what form this salvation will take. We simply have to try to surrender a self-centred narrative, in order to allow a divine, inclusive narrative to emerge.

This element of surrender, combined with an attitude of openness when it comes to outcomes, is an essential feature of incarnational ministry of all kinds. It also helps us to stop looking at the past through rose-tinted spectacles. Human beings have always felt frustrated, incomplete, and struggled with an ever-present fear of failure. We have always been empty vessels waiting to be filled with divine grace, longing for union with God – to 'become participants in the divine nature' (2 Peter 1.4).

However, we cannot simply override human nature: our suffering, our sense of incompleteness, our flaws, and our profound repression of the knowledge of our own death. We can only attempt to live honestly and humbly with the reality of our condition. A mass disaster such as the Grenfell fire is a sobering reminder of the terrible fragility of our existence, and a rebuke to facile affirmations of faith – such as, 'God is in control'.

In plumbing the depths of emptiness, even to the point of despair, Christ performed an action that existentially paralleled the Harrowing of Hell. He descended into a hell within each human being, a place of lostness and desolation, in order to lead us back up to the light.

This movement from the depths and back up to the heights is recorded in the verses that follow from the passage quoted above:

> Therefore God also highly exalted him
> and gave him the name
> that is above every name,
> so that at the name of Jesus
> every knee should bend,
> in heaven and on earth and under the earth,
> and every tongue should confess
> that Jesus Christ is Lord,
> to the glory of God the Father.
> (Letter of Paul to the Philippians 2.9–11)

Speaking truth to power

Jesus' injunction to be a good neighbour is only part of his teaching. Luke's Gospel tells us that from the moment Jesus entered public ministry, he assumed the prophetic mantle. As Jesus stood up in his home synagogue in Nazareth, to read passages from Isaiah, in which the prophet proclaims that the Spirit of the Lord is upon him, because he is anointed, 'to bring good news to the poor ... to proclaim release to the captives and recovery of sight to the blind, to let the oppressed go free, to proclaim the year of the Lord's favour', he adds, 'Today this scripture has been fulfilled in your hearing' (Luke 4.18–21).

From the very beginning, Jesus was driven to challenge exploitation. Even so, a passage towards the end of Matthew's Gospel is a shocking indictment of hypocrisy and the abuse of power by religious leaders. In Matthew 23, the repeated incantation of, 'woe to you, scribes and Pharisees, hypocrites', woven through 14 devastating verses, builds to a memorable lament over Jerusalem:

'Jerusalem, Jerusalem, the city that kills the prophets and stones those who are sent to it! How often have I desired to gather your children together as a hen gathers her brood under her wings, and you were not willing! See, your house is left to you, desolate. For I tell you, you will not see me again until you say, "Blessed is the one who comes in the name of the Lord."'
(Matthew 23.37–39)

This assault on the religious hierarchy – together with the concluding lament – clarifies key aspects of Jesus' own teaching. He came to heal, to liberate us from oppressive burdens, and with a radical message of equality before God. It is striking that he describes himself here as a 'hen'. The prophetic role was nurturing and motherly, and is illustrated through a homely agricultural image.

The themes of service and humility are reinforced elsewhere in the Gospels – and nowhere more strikingly than in John's account of the Last Supper, when Jesus adopts the position of someone of low social status: washing the feet of the disciples, and calling on them to do the same (John 13.13–15). The action of foot washing, repeated at the Maundy Thursday Eucharist, has probably done more to underline the centrality of service than any number of sermons. Symbolic action so often speaks louder than words.

Jesus attacks those who pursue status and wealth, and in highlighting the corruption of an entire infrastructure predicts its demise. In this, he stands in a prophetic tradition stretching back hundreds of years. The beginning of Isaiah (1.1–17) is one of many instances where we are told that the only way to a restored relationship with God is through a renewed commitment to justice, and to care for the exploited and vulnerable. If the poor are abused, religious observance is a sham.

When we talk today about pastoral care, we sometimes isolate it from political or social action. In the Hebrew Scriptures, prophets denounce injustice, cite the condition of the weakest in society (widows, orphans, foreigners), as part of a call to the nation to return to God – often in the face of impending devastation. Pastoral and political themes form an appeal for a renewed righteousness. Only when this happens will the nation restore its relationship with God, and receive God's blessing.

In his own time, Jesus was widely seen as a prophet (Matthew 16.13–14). However, the role of prophet is only one aspect of Jesus' identity. He is the Messiah, the 'anointed one', who will rule justly over Israel.

Jesus' role as 'ruler' or 'king' is highlighted from the moment of his birth. Matthew tells how the wise men came to Jerusalem, looking for the child who has been born king of the Jews. Herod responds with fear at the prospect of a 'shepherd king' after the model of David, as foretold by the prophets (Matthew 2.1–6).

The kingdom of God is an elusive term, which embraces both the present and the future. Jesus tells the Pharisees that, 'the kingdom of God is among you' (Luke 17.21), but goes on to say that 'the Son of Man' will be revealed in the devastation to come (17.22–30). The kingdom of God is both 'here and now' and 'not yet' – as it is for us today.

But while Jesus is a king, he is also a servant and a prophet who struggles against oppression; and the Gospel of John drives home the point that his kingship is expressed through his crucifixion. Pilate has a sign attached to the cross:

> There they crucified him, and with him two others, one on either side, with Jesus between them. Pilate also had an inscription written and put on the cross. It read, 'Jesus of Nazareth, the King of the Jews.' Many of the Jews read this inscription, because the place where Jesus was crucified was near the city; and it was written in Hebrew, in Latin, and in Greek. Then the chief priests of the Jews said to Pilate, 'Do not write, "The King of the Jews", but, "This man said, I am King of the Jews."' Pilate answered, 'What I have written I have written.'
> (John 19.18–22)

Jesus' identity as a prophet – who is also a healer, a teacher, and a servant king – helps us to understand the purpose of the church. A willingness to 'speak truth to power' is an essential feature of Christian witness. Jesus' passion and death stand in judgement over churches that collude with injustice in any form whatsoever.

The idea that the church inherits a prophetic calling was strengthened by the Grenfell Tower disaster. When a publicly owned building is consumed by a raging fire, and when that same building stands for months as a tomb and as a site of trauma, the church is required to resource itself from Jesus' fervour and authority.

In 1982, when I began training for ordained ministry, it was still quite common to hear people say that 'politics and religion don't mix'. At the same time, the Church of England was routinely referred to as the 'Tory Party at prayer'. This changed in 1985, with the publication of *Faith in the City*, a report written by the Archbishop of Canterbury's Commission on Urban Areas.

The controversy surrounding the report – some alleged that its authors were communists – indicated that the Church of England had found a new voice. The plight of those trapped in inner city deprivation was powerfully articulated in the public realm. *Faith in the City* helped create a space for faith leaders to speak about poverty and inequality, international development and our stewardship of the planet.

We talk now of 'theology in the public square', and the church understands ever more clearly that it has both a right and a duty to address concerns we face, as one nation among others. In this respect, the international leadership of the Papacy is a matter of supreme importance; Pope Francis has become an extraordinarily effective advocate for justice and compassion.

Recent political developments have shown that many people feel both angry and helpless in face of globalization. Creating a connection between people and their governments is now an urgent political task.

Parish ministry gives credibility to those who speak for the church about social justice. This is in its own small but significant way a step towards providing the type of linkage between communities and government that Western democracies often lack.

Faith communities are locally grounded, and yet have access to a more visible public platform. In situations where they have worked hard to establish credibility and trust, they can help with processes of mediation – for example, in South Africa's post-apartheid Truth and Reconciliation Commission. As we saw in the aftermath of the Grenfell fire, they can also help the powerful to hear the voices of the weak. Of course, they do not do this alone. In order to be effective, they must work in partnership with others: humbly, and from a desire to serve.

The entire infrastructure of 'national engagement' – all the way up to conversations with government, and high-profile services in cathedrals and abbeys – is ultimately justified by what the church does in its parishes. Without a meaningful commitment to an inclusive local ministry, it might hold onto its buildings, and its tokens of power and prestige, but it would lack authenticity.

Yet the Church of England is now at a point where it needs to think very carefully about how to protect its ground-level activity. As it faces serious questions about its future, it needs to decide how committed it is to remaining the Church 'of England', or whether it is content to drift towards being the Anglican Church 'in England'.

At senior levels, the imaginative energy of the past few years has been gathered around one particular concept of mission. In an attempt to reach new people in new ways, the Church of England has subtly downgraded the type of embedded, inclusive, 'alongside', incarnational parish ministry that provides a rationale for its status as the Established Church. Are we clear about what parishes have to offer in the twenty-first century? Or are they principally seen as an inheritance from the past, with a long, interesting and sometimes illustrious history, but serving no clear purpose today? Are parish clergy right at times to feel disregarded, as if their ministry is second-best – not really contributing to the big picture, necessary but rather dull? These and similar questions represent the proverbial elephant in the church.

With declining congregations, structural reorganization is clearly necessary. Those responsible for addressing this problem have a huge challenge, and some difficult choices. They deserve both our respect and our prayers, as they undertake a complex and at times no doubt dispiriting task. However, many at parish level also feel dispirited: unable to generate a sufficient level of attendance to make them appear 'successful', and at the same time forced to shoulder an often expensive architectural burden, on behalf of both the church and the wider community.

In this context, we need to find a gentler language of mutual respect, affirmation and support. We need to be liberated from oppressive models of success, driven by a self-punishing urge to achieve unrealistic outcomes. The Church of England will only find a purposeful and sustainable way forward if there is a concerted and committed attempt to engage with emotional realities at every level, from parishes upwards.

In particular, poor parishes need to be freed from the idea that they are a financial drain that the church can no longer afford. It is so easy for those ministering in disadvantaged areas to internalize the message that they are the ecclesiastical equivalent of what some in the media savagely label as 'benefit scroungers'. Given such spiteful stereotyping, those working and worshipping in poor parishes need to be told that they make a vital contribution to the church, and are helping to shape its vision.

One way of doing this is to set alongside the current – and important – emphasis on evangelism a complementary emphasis on service and prophecy. Through pastoral care and the ministry of presence, parish churches become hard-wired into a wider community. There will always be occasions when a parish church emerges as an important focal point and resource. This happened at St Clement's and other places of worship on 14 June 2017. But the church's contribution is not limited to traumatic events.

Congregations generally expect their clergy to have something intelligent to say about wider developments. They expect to be supported in their attempts to relate faith to a range of social as well as personal issues. Service and prophecy are a natural and inevitable part of a lively parish church; and often result in faith-based community initiatives.

At the same time, those occupying high-level positions are currently able to draw on ground-level experience to contribute to wider debates about public policy. However, the Church of England needs to decide whether it is fully committed to maintaining – or better still, extending – its position on the national stage. If so, then it needs to ensure it continues to speak affirmatively about traditional parish ministry, looking to promote good examples of community engagement.

Perhaps it should now begin using historic reserves much more extensively, to re-energize parishes with very high levels of deprivation – especially in dioceses facing a financial crisis. If we are indeed at a critical juncture – as some suggest we are – then the Church of England needs to reinvent itself. It is hard to see how it will be able to do this without a significant investment in the social gospel.

But most fundamentally of all, we are challenged to embrace something far greater than organizational survival. While each of us has a duty to exercise responsible institutional stewardship, we must constantly bear two things in mind: first, that for Jesus the kingdom of God was a central proclamation, and second, that his earthly throne was the cross.

FINDING WORDS

What does it mean to 'find words for Grenfell'?

At this point we have to acknowledge frankly that it is probably impossible for any individual to 'find words for Grenfell' – especially so soon after the fire. Yet testimonies given directly after traumatic events have their own value. They speak with urgency and a quality of bewilderment and pain it is important to capture, even though later assessments may offer a more complete overview.

The first part of this book sets out the sequence of events as I saw them from 14 June to the end of 2017. 'Finding words' in this context means 'description'. My knowledge is limited, but it contributes something to the historical record.

The second part presents some interconnected theological reflections, gathered around an experience of parish ministry. Here I have sought to 'find words for the church'. The Grenfell Tower fire helped me to focus these thoughts, but they have a deeper source, and wider implications. The incarnation of Christ is at the heart of an approach to ministry and mission that is at once pastoral and prophetic, personal and political, and is developed through two further themes: 'theosis' or divinization, and the kingdom of God.

This line of thought stems from a point of view that has been reinforced by the Grenfell fire: that our current proclamation of the gospel is far too individualistic. One of the most significant outcomes from the disaster has been a new valuing of solidarity. The volunteer support in the first few days of the disaster, the partnerships between organizations, key interventions such as the St Paul's Cathedral National Memorial Service, and the mutual support between residents reflect a longing for neighbourliness that seems to be deeper and more wide-spread than many of us previously thought.

Yet when we speak theologically of 'salvation' we invariably focus on the individual. The public affirmation of belief, a commitment to a personal relationship with God in Christ, and a developed understanding of what this means are all signs of a maturing faith. But too often we stop there.

Somehow we have to find a way to enter more fully into our communal and historical identity: rooted in 2,000 years of Christian witness and ministry, yet without succumbing to isolationism or triumphalism. We need to be more completely ourselves – not just as a collection of individuals loved by Jesus but as a community – while at the same time becoming ever more connected to communities that journey alongside us, and with which we are called to work in partnership.

Inevitably, we find ourselves moving back and forth between the ideas that shape and order our understanding of God and the world we inhabit, and the raw data of life as it is lived. In the best case, each informs the other in a process of continual enrichment. But this process is by its nature open-ended, and in any case it would be futile to attempt to bring a book about a mass disaster to a neat conclusion. This last section is therefore much less linear than the previous two sections. We search for 'words' but we do not necessarily find them; and even when we do find them they do not necessarily form a satisfactory whole. However, the important thing is that we search.

The short chapters that now follow address different aspects of the fire and its consequences, almost in the form of linked meditations, and not necessarily in chronological order. They are perhaps best seen as 'These fragments I have shored against my ruins', to borrow a line from T. S. Eliot's *The Waste Land*. Given the catastrophic nature of the Grenfell fire, I have chosen to end the book on a more tentative note than some may wish, and I have avoided the spurious consolations of false hope, as an affront to those who died or continue to suffer.

Having said this, the recovery of hope will be a vital part of communal healing in North Kensington. For many local people, the desire to enjoy life once more has been accompanied by a feeling of guilt and a sense of betrayal.

By contrast, affirmations of hope that do not trivialize pain are both sustaining and liberating. They give us a new language, and help us to navigate our way around a psychological and emotional impasse. Traditional hymnody has such affirmations in abundance, and perhaps nowhere more economically than in the great hymn by Isaac Watts, based on Psalm 90:

O God, our help in ages past,
Our hope for years to come,
Our shelter from the stormy blast,
And our eternal home.

This lucid hymn, with its sparing and precise deployment of imagery, expresses both emotional turmoil and a longing for rest in God. Because it is not cluttered by biographical detail, and because it speaks from another century – while looking even further back to 'ages past' – it provides us with an opportunity to speak to God in a way that is personal and yet also part of a living tradition. In singing this hymn – and others of equal quality, old and new – we form a connection with Christians who have lived and died before us, and who nourish us by their wisdom, integrity and artistic ability.

Universal fragility

The Grenfell fire shows other disasters in a new light. On 14 June, the media described a 'Blitz spirit', as Londoners rallied round to provide care and support. In the days that followed, I found myself wondering about those who actually lived through the Blitz: the terror of the bombardment, the frantic attempts to quench fires, the appalling task of removing dead bodies from bombed buildings. This was before counselling services were deemed necessary or readily available, and anyway the country was at war. There were more immediate priorities and very few resources.

Equally, many combatants saw and heard things they could never describe to their families. Psychologists tell us that trauma creates strong bonds between those who suffer together, while undermining their capacity to connect with those on the outside. Throughout the summer, there was a sharp divide between North Kensington and the surrounding areas. Only a short distance away, people were sitting at bars and cafes, enjoying the sunshine.

At its best, the media had an important bridge role, helping convey news to the wider world: to build sympathy and rally support – in part, because it was relatively easy to get to North Kensington, repeatedly and at short notice. But would the coverage have been as widespread if the disaster had occurred far away from London, or from regional TV centres? Without it, would the general public have been so engaged?

The carnage inflicted by Hurricane Irma on the Caribbean and parts of the United States in late August and early September 2017 occurred at the same time as floods in South Asia. At least 134 people died as a result of the hurricane, whereas over 1,200 died in South Asia. Far greater attention was paid to the hurricane, as it was much easier to cover the disaster in the southern United States, and to tell the human stories that mattered so much – and, of course, those affected spoke English. Predictably, the media is driven by what it sees as the level of public interest. But this has the pervasive effect of reinforcing the assumption that some lives matter more than others.

This is not to suggest that the media should not have reported extensively on the terrible losses inflicted by Hurricane Irma, or the Grenfell Tower fire. By and large, after the intrusive first few days, North Kensington residents saw the value of the ongoing media interest; it enabled others to understand and empathize.

The media helped to show the human face of suffering; and from the autumn onwards, some high-quality documentaries were released. Equally, those who were lost

– mainly from immigrant communities – were often seen in touching family photographs. The victims looked relaxed, sometimes happy. Children posed for their parents. The intimate, domestic nature of these photographs captured life in North Kensington for so many.

At one point, it felt as if the anger we saw from the summer onwards was beginning to redefine the public perception of the area. But those photographs told another story. They spoke of ordinary people getting on with their lives: taking their children to school, going to work, enjoying family celebrations. They had a powerful impact locally: pinned to fences and trees, hung on railings, taped to walls and lampposts ... face after face after face ... for long after anyone could plausibly claim the victims were simply missing. The photographs stayed up for weeks, before being gradually and quietly removed.

Shortly after the fire, someone rather callously observed to me that at least those in the tower and the bereaved were from countries where suffering is endemic: 'At least they're used to it.' In fact, many will have arrived in this country carrying significant emotional burdens. Many will have been far more wounded, far less resilient, and with far weaker personal support systems. Poverty and exile invariably intensify suffering.

What would it take for us to extend the sympathy we felt for those traumatized by the Grenfell fire outward to poorer countries, where lives seem so much more disposable?

The trauma that endures

In the months after the Grenfell fire, people began to ask the question, 'How are things in North Kensington now?' This was a very difficult question to answer. No one person has an overview of 'the community'.

The most that could be said was that the situation was ongoing: that, months later, for many people the situation felt no better and that some would continue to struggle with their trauma for years, and possibly the rest of their lives. On a practical level, rehousing survivors proved difficult, for a variety of reasons, and even six months after the fire, only a small number had left temporary accommodation. Meanwhile, the blackened tower loomed over the neighbourhood. Imagine leaving your home each day and passing the mangled car in which those you love have been killed. That was what the tower represented for many local people.

Psychologists tell us that those who suffer from post-traumatic stress disorder feel trapped, unable to move forward in any meaningful way. Events in the present trigger the trauma. Sights and sounds have the capacity to collapse time. The traumatized may experience night-mares, disassociation and the recurrence of distressing images, or they may feel numbed and dead inside. Either way, they are dominated by the past.

Counselling support was soon available, but some found the process of registering for help alienating and worry-ing. How would this information be used? Why should they trust healthcare workers, when they had been so badly let down by local government? Others were simply not used to talking about themselves, or found it too difficult to surmount the barriers of language or culture. Still others found talking about the fire too upsetting. Perhaps they were not yet ready to speak about their experiences. Perhaps they never would be.

Although important, talking therapy is only one form of trauma treatment. Art and drama also have a signifi-cant contribution to make, in part because it is now widely accepted that traumatic recurrences are not acts of remembering, but of reliving. In a discussion with someone involved in a trauma project, I found it helpful to explore the connection between the bodily nature of trauma and the therapeutic qualities of worship. We cer-tainly saw this at the Parish Mass at St Clement's on the Sunday after the fire.

The sense of solidarity apparent from the opening prayer onwards … The oscillation between anger and grief … The release of feeling as candles were lit, and hymns were sung … Weeping, embracing … The encounter with

Christ in the Eucharist ... The compassionate touch of others, in the laying on of hands and anointing ... All within the safe and containing structure of the liturgy.

Those responsible for leading the worship felt these things to an extent, but our experience was more limited. We were primarily agents in a process of care and encounter, acting on behalf of others.

My experience of sacramental healing came four weeks after the fire, at the local Catholic church: St Francis of Assisi. Although invited to robe by the parish priest, I had no liturgical responsibilities, and for that I was grateful. As an Anglican, I could not receive Holy Communion, but the celebrant, Bishop John Wilson, laid his hand on my head and blessed me. Exhausted, needy, overwhelmed, as yet in no position to process what I had witnessed and shared with others, I experienced in that simple action a profound affirmation of God's love.

The emotional and spiritual connection I felt in that church was magnified by the nature of the worship. In the Eucharist, Christ's brokenness enables us to approach our own brokenness. His giving enables us to give. Communion is affirmed. We are drawn into the life of God. A blessing is received.

It may be that the most significant aspect of this story is that I was able to be vulnerable because this was not my church. I was a guest. For a short period, I was released from all responsibilities and this was deeply therapeutic.

Who speaks?

Right from the start, the tower survivors made it clear that they wanted to be considered separately from other evacuees – and so they formed Grenfell United and smaller survivor organizations. Residents associations also became important forums for discussion. These were closed meetings, to which guests could be invited.

It was difficult for those outside North Kensington to interpret the anger seen at public meetings, or at demonstrations. Some took it as a sign of outside political interference, but this was to underestimate the extent to which virtually everyone in the area felt betrayed. Most were convinced that a catastrophe on this scale would never have happened to a middle-class population, and wanted to see statutory authorities – and individuals – held to account. Some expressed their anger externally, while others carried it around within themselves.

There was a widespread loss of trust in authority. Many were sceptical that the Inquiry would get to the truth, and the knowledge that they faced a long wait for any kind of justice compounded a debilitating sense of helplessness.

Broken connections and a sense of being overwhelmed –
two classic signs of trauma – were a persistent feature of
the emotional landscape in Notting Dale. The impact on
residents' mental health was immense.

Even so, the general principle was clear: we should only
speak from our own experience. In the immediate aftermath of the disaster, many voices and agendas emerged.
Those living and working in North Kensington were
sensitized to the issue of exploitation. They noticed when
an individual or organization from outside edged into the
camera, or sought to capitalize on the disaster – whether
for financial, political or personal reasons. Self-interested
'help' was experienced as a form of abuse.

Such a shocking and preventable tragedy should change
our society for the better. It should rekindle a commitment
to justice and the common good. It should regenerate
social unity. But in order to be of real assistance, we need
to be as honest as possible about our motives. We need
to ask the question, 'Whose interests am I serving?'

Speaking can be cathartic, as I discovered when a poem I
wrote was published in *The Guardian* in September 2017
– and that can be found at the end of this book. I was
then asked to read the poem aloud in various contexts.
At each stage, I tried to emphasize that I was speaking
from a limited perspective, as one who lives fairly close
to Grenfell Tower but not immediately beside it, and as
one helper among many. The poem was based on my

own experiences, and the experiences others had shared with me, but like everyone who spoke in public, I was under an obligation to ensure that I was attempting to speak *on behalf* of those who suffered the most, and not *instead* of them. I trod the difficult line of advocacy. The opportunity to speak underlined how important it was to have a voice; and yet so many had yet to feel heard.

Towards a new narrative

Through the visceral expression of lament, through acts of remembrance, of telling – and retelling – our experiences in safe places, and through the knowledge that we are being heard, it may be possible in time for a new narrative to emerge: of a broken life lived on.

After any significant loss the journey to recovery will be long, and even when it eventually arrives healing may well be partial. We may be permanently wounded. The dead we have loved may remain part of who we are. We may hold within ourselves an empty space that will never be filled. Consequently, prayers for the dead meet an enduring emotional need. Many of us have a strong desire to pray for those we have loved, and love still, wherever they may be.

In the wake of a mass disaster, there is a need for repeated acts of remembrance: to tell the story, to be heard, and to connect with those who have been lost. And yet what happened in Notting Dale beggared both belief and description. It could not be fitted into any normal frame of reference – at least not in a prosperous city such as

London, with all its apparent safeguards. How can we get our heads – let alone our hearts – around what happened? How can we find the language to express our grief at the loss of so many people in unimaginably terrifying circumstances?

And yet a new narrative will have to be constructed, in time, of one kind or another. Part of this narrative will – we hope – be political and social. The Grenfell Tower fire showed us something about our society many had not seen before, or at least not in this way: a lack of attention, a heartlessness, an absence of respect, of care, a reluctance to listen, especially to those living under the stigma of social housing. Equally, many on the estates in North Kensington saw something they had been unwilling or unable to acknowledge: that the neglect of their living conditions was not 'normal', and could not be justified. This new narrative has yet to emerge. As we have seen from the continuing anger at public meetings, there is still too much trauma to be processed.

Grenfell Tower has become a potent symbol of neglect, incompetence and injustice. Will it change our society for the better? It is far too soon to tell. But at some stage we will need to move on to constructive dialogue and engagement. If this does not happen, the symbolic language will become debased, and turn into rhetoric. The problem is that, as I write this, no one wants to betray the symbol; and so there is no clear way of resolving conflict and building trust.

The pale spire of the Notting Hill Methodist church, seen against the blackened Grenfell Tower, has become for many a sign of hope. Places of worship have an important place on a symbolic map, along with public spaces, memorials and, most important of all, the Grenfell site itself. In time, all these will have to be woven into a new language of place, offering the possibility for renewal and hope. But it will take many years, and will require a determined commitment to reconciliation and cooperation.

Six-month anniversary

The Grenfell Tower National Memorial Service at St Paul's Cathedral on 14 December was an unusual act of remembrance. The number of those who died had only been given a month earlier.

The feelings of the bereaved were still raw – as they were for a large number of other residents and helpers, both in the Cathedral and watching it on television. Many found the service harrowing. Even so, it was widely agreed that it was therapeutic.

The service had been prepared with care and imagination. Cathedral clergy had made frequent trips to North Kensington, to meet local people, and to gather and share ideas. A background quality of deep, attentive listening was apparent throughout.

Key features included a specially made banner, of the green Grenfell heart, carried in by Fahim Mazhary of Al-Manaar Cultural Heritage Centre and Mosque, and Fr Gerard Skinner, of St Francis Assisi Catholic church. They were chosen because very many Muslims died, and the majority of Christian victims were Catholic. I will never forget the sight of the banner moving up the long aisle: seeming so small and fragile as it began its journey from the west end, in the huge, crowded Cathedral.

An oud was played, introducing a montage of voices captured during and after the fire; bringing back the first few weeks with horrifying directness. Many in the congregation wept. Some said afterwards that they wished they had been prepared for this element of the service. The montage was a risk, but most felt it had been one worth taking, because it gave the service the immediacy it needed.

The Al-Sadiq and Al-Zahra Schools Girls' Choirs sang beautifully 'Insha Allah' ('if God wills it'), and the Cathedral choir accompanied local schoolchildren with 'Somewhere', from *West Side Story*, as they scattered small green paper hearts on the dais.

The Bishop of Kensington's sermon addressed both the grief and the anger of residents, and alluded to the un-answered question of why warnings were 'unheeded'. His hope was that the United Kingdom would learn from the disaster: how to listen and to love. This vision of a deeper social unity was modelled in the beautifully crafted ser-vice, and could be seen in the diverse congregation.

While the service had a Christian framework, it was inclusive. Row after row was packed with Muslims

– many women, many in hijabs – all of whom seemed completely at home. Apart from the country's political leadership, there was a strong royal presence. The service was attended by the Prince of Wales, the Duchess of Cornwall, the Duke and Duchess of Cambridge and Prince Harry.

Superbly and sensitively filmed by the BBC, the service was an act of deep solidarity. The bereaved, survivors and other residents felt their pain was acknowledged by the nation. It was fitting that a mass disaster that six months earlier had called forth a 'Blitz spirit' of support was being marked in the Cathedral that during World War Two had been a symbol of national resilience; fitting too that this memorial service took its place alongside so many other acts of remembrance in the intervening years.

The St Paul's banner was carried back to Notting Hill Methodist church, and at 6.30 pm it was brought out for the evening's silent march. On the fourteenth day of each month since the fire, this act of commemoration began at the church, moved up to Ladbroke Grove, where firefighters respectfully formed a line, and made its way back down to Maxilla Walk, under the Westway flyover, for speeches. This format was changed in February 2018, when the march was extended outside North Kensington.

I had discussed the possibility of bringing along the banner with the march's organizers, but we were surprised to see that it was given pride of place at the front, among the bereaved and tower survivors. This demonstrated the high level of respect felt locally for the faith organizations, and how much the memorial service earlier that day was appreciated.

The St Paul's Cathedral service took place in the context of deep and continuing trauma. It felt more like a funeral than a memorial service. But like a funeral, it was an important step on a long journey to recovery, while powerfully articulating the need for far-reaching social change.

Stages along the way

For some, the St Paul's Memorial Service, and the silent march on 14 December, were something of a turning point, leading to an opportunity for rest over the vacation – while others found Christmas difficult.

From a church point of view, it was wonderful to have normal Christmas services, to reconnect with a familiar pattern. The darkness into which the Christ Child was born had a new resonance. We were reminded that the nativity has a resilient core, with the capacity to sustain us, even in situations of extreme pain.

The poem that ends this book reflected my state of mind over the summer of 2017. Its particular sense of powerlessness, of trauma relived, stayed with me until the end of November, when at public readings I began to discover that I no longer felt the words with such painful immediacy. It is perhaps no accident that this transition occurred near the 150th anniversary Mass at St Clement's church – on 26 November – when friends from over four decades gathered to celebrate what the church had meant to them. Naturally, we also looked further back: to the dedication of the church in 1867, and the heroic efforts of the Revd Alfred Dalgarno Robinson.

In his sermon, Michael Colclough, a former Bishop of Kensington, pictured Christ the King welcoming the founder of St Clement's into his eternal reward:

> Come, you that are blessed by my Father, inherit the kingdom prepared for you from the foundation of the world; for I was hungry in Notting Dale and you gave me food, I was thirsty in Notting Dale and you gave me something to drink, I was a stranger in Notting Dale and you welcomed me, I was naked in Notting Dale and you gave me clothing, I was sick in Notting Dale and you took care of me, and when I left Notting Dale to go to prison, you visited me.

In these moving words, the particularity of place was powerfully affirmed. At that moment, the kingdom of God felt very real, very present, very local. Heaven seemed to touch earth, as if we in our way each embodied the incarnation of Christ, here and now.

Our acts of compassion may feel insignificant, and we are all too often aware that we are not the people we wish to be. But our small offerings of love are part of a larger movement that we intermittently intuit, as over time, in the company of those with whom we live and work, we are taken up into the life of God.

Grasping what matters

This book has been a brief attempt to convey how badly residents were affected by the Grenfell Tower fire, how remarkably organizations have worked together, and how much there is still to do. It has also sought to offer a stress-tested rationale for parish ministry.

In a mass disaster, we glimpse how easily and profoundly we can be damaged, and how important it is to develop good channels of communication, from ground level all the way up to national government. Fatal failures in regulation, planning and governance have highlighted weaknesses in our democracy – and their impact on the most vulnerable in our society.

Commitment at the local level enables faith leaders to speak with conviction and authority about matters of public policy – a vitally important task following any emergency, and especially necessary in areas of deprivation, where the voices of the poor are frequently unheard. However, the task of realizing the kingdom of God in our midst is too ambitious to be undertaken alone. Effective social outreach, pastoral care, service and prophetic witness require a communal response. In the aftermath of the fire, we recognized our neighbours as our partners; and in our own vulnerability we saw the vulnerability of others.

The Grenfell disaster has shown us that worshipping communities have a significant capacity to elicit trust, to build bridges, to assist in conversation and mediation, and to become safe spaces for healing and advocacy. However, in order to serve in a crisis, they need to be in a state of readiness, with a record of authentic prior commitment.

At the same time, they need to be prepared for the cost such service will bring. Communal grief is exhausting. In this respect, I have seen the value of two things above all: the sacraments of the church, and the compassion of friends and neighbours.

Through earthquake, wind and fire

The emotional exhaustion experienced by Elijah in the first book of Kings after his confrontation with the priests of Baal, in the reign of the corrupt ruler Ahab (ninth century BC), is a fascinating biblical description of recovery from trauma.

After a public and dangerous test of the efficacy of his faith, in which God sends a fire to consume not only his sacrificial offerings, but also the altar, the dust around the altar and the water in outer trenches, Elijah has the prophets killed (1 Kings 18.38–40). However, this puts his life at risk. Jezebel, the wife of King Ahab, sends him a message that she intends to murder him.

Elijah flees to the wilderness, lies down beneath a broom tree, and sleeps. He is then woken twice by an angel, who touches him and urges him to eat cake baked on hot stones, and to drink the water he finds by his head, in order to have the strength to undertake a long journey. Forty days later he arrives at Mount Horeb, and shelters in a cave, which is where the word of the Lord comes to him:

> He said, 'Go out and stand on the mountain before the Lord, for the Lord is about to pass by.' Now there was a great wind, so strong that it was splitting mountains and breaking rocks in pieces before the Lord, but the Lord was not in the wind; and after the wind an earthquake, but the Lord was not in the earthquake; and after the earthquake a fire, but the Lord was not in the fire; and after the fire a sound of sheer silence.
> (1 Kings 19.11–12)

In this story of violent conflict, we see a gradually renewed capacity to function, leading to a re-entry into the public sphere. Initially, Elijah is terrified. In safety, he receives the nourishment he needs to journey on. Over a period of 40 days, he retreats to a sacred place. God tells him what he needs to do in order to ensure the political and spiritual regeneration of Israel. From his distress and exhaustion a new sense of direction emerges. The silence of the desert has been restorative.

This story of renewal has a New Testament parallel in the Acts of the Apostles. After the trauma of Christ's torture and agonizing death, the demoralized and frightened disciples have been encouraged by his resurrection appearances, and given a new sense of purpose through his ascension. They have begun to organize themselves, appointing Matthias in place of Judas.

On the day of Pentecost, a wind enters the house where they are gathered, tongues of fire rest on their heads, and they are filled with the Holy Spirit. They are propelled outside, to communicate across the barriers of language. Peter preaches the first Christian sermon, drawing on a visionary prophetic tradition from the Hebrew Scriptures, exemplified by the prophet Joel, proclaims the death and resurrection of Christ, and calls the hearers to repentance and baptism (Acts 1–2).

These two stories deploy the imagery of wind and fire differently – this imagery has uncomfortable resonances in North Kensington – but both speak of resilience, courage and a fresh momentum. In both cases, the central characters experience renewal, but they have been so badly wounded that their newly discovered confidence and determination is untainted by triumphalism.

They remind us that we cannot rush ahead to healing. There are no short cuts. We must give ourselves space to process what we have experienced, and we must allow the grace of God to do its work in its own time. Only then can we take the next step, in the hope that God will accompany us and guide us forward.

A continuing presence

An extensive process of consultation will be needed before any decisions can be taken about the tower site. The fire has raised huge issues about social housing policy and funding; and it will take years before these are addressed – if at all. We are in the very early stages of a lengthy and difficult process.

Places of worship, schools and community centres, embedded in their neighbourhoods, will continue to do their work long after the media spotlight has moved away. Their commitment to support and empower residents is for the long term; and yet in a culture that prizes high-profile interventions and radical change, they are all too easily taken for granted.

Decisive action may often be necessary to fix endemic problems, and can sometimes be creative, opening up new ways to better performance. We would have liked to see much more disaster planning and preparation by the council before the Grenfell fire, and much more decisive action afterwards. The Prime Minister's intervention on 17 June came as a great relief. It provided momentum, and restored a degree of confidence in the system. At least we had the feeling that something was being done. However, her undertaking that evacuees would be rehoused in three weeks was wildly unrealistic, and unhelpfully raised expectations. In this respect, the local council was set up to fail. Decisive action is not always positive.

We can only hope that the government and local authorities have learned from the Grenfell fire, and are now committed to more rigorous disaster planning. To be effective, these plans will have to include community organizations, with their on-the-ground presence.

Equally, faith communities need to improve their own levels of preparedness. From 2003, when I was in the East End, I initiated and led the development of ecumenical Major Incident Teams. Relationships with the emergency services and council officers were well established, and clergy were well trained. This planning proved invaluable two years later, during the terrorist bombings of London's public transport system on 7 July 2005. But without a valued and resourced parish system, we cannot make this type of contribution.

Over the past 20 years, it has been said with increasing frequency that the inherited parochial model of the Church of England is broken and cannot be fixed. Sometimes the Day of Pentecost is recruited to this point of view, and offered as a model for renewal and growth.

The Holy Spirit, some say, comes with wind and fire, sweeping aside old, ineffective ways of doing things.

Yet the Pentecost narrative needs to be read in context. In the first place, it was preceded by a recovery period, in which the disciples were able to process their distress, and to regroup. Second, they would have been unable to obliterate their own past. The tradition that Peter wanted to be crucified upside down, because he did not feel worthy of the same execution as the Lord he had denied, reflects the insight that trauma lives on. His sense of guilt may well have been shared by other disciples. Moreover, the first Christian community would have struggled with their expulsion from synagogues and the temple at Jerusalem. In this period of astonishingly creative change, many would have been deeply wounded. It should be no surprise that it was a later convert – Paul – who came to shape the identity of the new religion in a new, Gentile world. Even so, the testimony and experiences of the apostles would have been formative – not least because they had known Jesus personally, and had suffered with him.

The Grenfell disaster helps us to value and cherish continuity: to recognize the necessity of working to build and rebuild the kingdom of God at parish level. And yet no one in North Kensington is a hero. In the words of one faith leader: 'We didn't choose to be here, and we weren't chosen for our abilities. Plenty of other people could have done just as well as we did. It was just our bad luck that it was us. It was just the randomness of this terrible event.'

It is impossible for a book of this sort, written so soon after a disaster such as the Grenfell fire, to end on anything other than a sombre note. The poem that follows bears the imprint of the horrifying summer of 2017. It was all I could manage to say at that point, and from a very limited perspective. Even our best attempts at expression fall short of the reality of experience: in the final reckoning, we are only ever left with little more 'Than dust on our lips'.

In the end, no one person is capable of 'finding words for Grenfell', and yet attempts must be made: to bear witness, however imperfectly, to both the scale of the trauma, and the resilience of the community that endured it.

14 June 2017

I

In the network of streets, divided by cordons
And beyond them all the barrier
Of jammed cars
There appeared, as if from nowhere
Hundreds, no make that thousands
Of bottles of water
Passed from hand to hand
As the sun beat down on exposed heads
And sweaty backs
On the car-less streets
In the blanket of heat
We couldn't kick off
Trapped in a dream
From which we couldn't escape
Because it wasn't a dream.

We hardly slept for days.

II

The crowd that night from the neighbouring blocks
The finger blocks
Forced to watch
Lights at the windows
Torches
Of those who were still alive
For the time being
Signalling
Desperate faint hope
Until floor by floor
The darkness snuffed them out.

Imagine fire leaping up the building
Imagine cries for help
Imagine screams
Imagine the staircase
The crowded and all too soon
Impassable
Single staircase
Imagine the condition of the bodies
They managed to recover
Imagine not knowing
For days on end
Whether relatives or friends were still alive
And then still 'not knowing'

… No body to lay to rest.

III

And what about the firefighter who wasn't even there
Driven to recount
What people sound like
When they miss the mark
The sound which is like no other
The distinctive and unforgettable sound
Of impact
When a body hits the ground?

And what about the firefighters
Who were there that night
In the early hours
Of the fourteenth of June
Who kitted up
And went straight in
Crawling along the floor beneath the smoke
Reaching up grasping hands guiding survivors out

Who haven't yet recovered?

IV

It's impossible to picture the street
As it was, an ordinary street

At the fringe of the Carnival route
When the Tower stood out

In its smart new cladding
When persistent prophetic warnings

Fell with a thud on deaf ears
Before 'tenants' became 'survivors'

Trapped
In distant hotel rooms

Unable to move forward, or to go back.

V

A lifeless black block
A grave vessel

Only the visible remains
Have so far been removed
To a location some say
Is not so far away
Where the teeth the bones the body parts
Are being identified for burial
Or to complete the process of cremation
And now we've started we can't stop
Thinking about the location some say
Is not so far away
Where the process the procedures
God almighty the scale of it
The eye for detail
The expertise on which we depend
To deliver truth prosecutions
Blind to authority blind to power
Justice
For Grenfell.

What's 'justice'?

Moving upward
So slowly
Fingertip sifting
They won't be finished until Christmas
They say, Christmas 2017 that is
Remember the year
Invisible from out here
But in there, up there
Within that silent perforated tomb
With its single staircase
Its devastated rooms
Open to the sky
Picking their way through matter
Organic and inorganic
Matter
Mingled
Matter
Up twenty three flights of stairs
To the distant upper floors
The building shifts
Blocks are evacuated
But the movement is well within
'The usual parameters'.

What's 'usual'?

VI

Poor souls
That's what people call them
In letter after letter

Stripped of bodies
Of faces
Unrecognizable

Except perhaps to God
No flesh anchor
To secure them

Naked, exposed
How will they find God
Without a body

Drifting alone
Between stars
In the empty black ocean?

And the poor souls who survived them
Stripped of so much
Cast adrift

We call them 'survivors'
A label to hold them in place
But they have no place

To call 'home'
Buffeted by …
… Absence …

VII

St Clement's church
Packed out at the parish mass
On the first Sunday after the fire
Friends and strangers
Standing so still
For the opening prayer
Listening so intently
To the angry searing sermon
Clergy so rarely preach
Sermons like that
Which is why so many people wrote to me afterwards
   to say
It almost restored their faith
In Christianity
Almost

Friends and strangers
Who wanted to stand
Alongside one another
In silence
In prayer in grief in remembrance
Who wanted to light a candle
Who went forward so swiftly
To the stations around the church
Who wept
At the sight of small flames in trays of sand

Ironic, don't you think – 'flames-fire'?

Not at all

Those candles represented life
They represented pain
They represented hope
However fragile

And there was energy that day
We held it together
Anger respect release you name it
It was all there and between us we made a difference

And the Eucharist was deep
In a way words cannot capture
Because you cannot capture Christ
You cannot capture the Holy Spirit

But now ... now ...
We're small and disconnected and tired
And as powerless as we've ever been
And coming together feels almost too raw
And everywhere you look
There are people walking around
In a daze

Haunted by ghosts
By images
They try to shut out

And there it is
Right there
The dead black block
We see it
Each morning

Filled with debris and dust
When so much was driven out by the fire
And carried away by the wind

It's all around us
In the air we breathe
In our tormented nights
In our dreams

And the giant ruptured
Incinerator
Is there to greet us
As always
When we awake.

VIII

Debris
Flickering shadows
In the mind

The dead are present
Even when we forget them
Even in the words we fail to speak

But when concerned observers
Publish words of anger or distress
Attempting to be the voice

Of those who have lost the most
We're left with little more
Than dust on our lips.

Personal acknowledgements

With heartfelt thanks for the many relationships that have been a source of joy, resilience and practical support: friends, colleagues and family; those in the two parish congregations and more widely in the Diocese of London, as well as new friends made through ecumenical and interfaith collaboration.

I am especially grateful for the help given to me in very pressurized circumstances by the team at Canterbury Press, and to Matthew Barrett and Nicolas Wheeler who at various times have offered me invaluable journalistic advice.

Above all, I must record here my love and deep gratitude to my wife Julie Hare, and my two daughters Emily and Charlotte Everett-Hare.

Acknowledgement of sources

The Rt Revd Michael Colclough, 'Sermon for the 150th Anniversary of St Clement Notting Dale', 26 November 2017.

The ClementJames Centre, 'Winter Newsletter', December 2017.

William Blake, 'And did those feet in ancient time', in the Preface to *Milton: A Poem in Two Books*, 1808.

Pope Francis, *Evangelii Gaudium* (*The Joy of the Gospel*), Catholic Truth Society, 2013.

T. S. Eliot, 'The Waste Land', in *The Waste Land and Other Poems*, Faber & Faber, 2002.

Isaac Watts, 'Our God, our help in ages past', 1719.

'14 June 2017' was first published by *The Guardian*, September 2017.